# IMAZIGHAN

## PATRICIA WARREN

LIFEJOURNEY
BOOKS

LifeJourney Books™ is an imprint of Chariot Family Publishing,
a div. of David C. Cook Publishing Co.
David C. Cook Publishing Co., Elgin, Illinois 60120
David C. Cook Publishing Co., Weston, Ontario
Nova Distribution Ltd., Newton Abbot, England

IMAZIGHAN
©1993 by Patricia Warren

Cover design by Turnbaugh & Associates
Interior Design by Glass House Graphics
Edited by Susan Brinner

First Printing, 1993
Printed in the United States of America
97 96 95 94 93   5  4  3  2  1

CIP Applied for.
ISBN 0-78140-940-3

To God be the glory.
May my words be channels that the
Word of Life flows through.

# ▦▦▦▦▦▦ Prologue ▦▦▦▦▦▦

If I pulled far enough sideways against the neck ring, I could just manage a glimpse of cold desert stars through the slit in the crumbling rock wall. But those tiny pricks of light kept blurring and dancing, so I tried refocusing on Shay, or at least in the direction of the shallow panting that rattled over there on the far side of our inky cell. I wished I could rub my tired, gritty eyes.

*Dear Father, I only asked for some relief from the monotony, the drudgery of my same old routines. I didn't ask to be mixed up in something like this!*

Was it only a few short weeks ago that I'd been dragging through impatient days and sleepless nights, feeling both stuck and adrift?

*Lord, please don't let it be too late to go back to my blessed life of mundane service—to go home.*

# 1

Waaay down upon the Swaneeee River . . . *Pop! Pop!*
"My turn, Daddy, my turn!"
"Do a really awesome, humongous one, Dad."

Joe, my sweet Joe, was supposed to be down the hall helping the girls finish up their bath and get into their pjs. But from the off-key, enthusiastic singing punctuated by loud pops and giggles, I suspected he was putting on a soap-bubble show, not scrubbing backs.

As I stood at the kitchen sink with my hands in the last of the greasy dishwater—the dishwasher was broken again—I was simultaneously being treated to fractured renditions of "Twinkle, Twinkle Little Star," complete with multiple squawking starts, stops, and mutterings. This painful descant was provided by J.D., Joseph Lowe Daniels, Jr., age ten, who had inherited his father's jet black curls, but looked out on the world through serious, smoky gray eyes like mine. Holed up in his favorite alcove off the laundry porch, my eldest son was practicing his saxophone piece for the school band.

He is a quiet, reliable boy rocketing much too quickly toward adolescence. The sax is only the latest in a long line of varied interests. Like me, he's always wanted to try his hand at many different academic subjects, all kinds of sports, and arts. J.D. confronts life with intelligence and his own brand of enthusiasm. Unfortunately, he also desires to be immediately perfect at anything he tries.

"No, no, really, Guy. Yeah, I'm doing mine on our new kittens. Hey, one's so radical it's . . . ."

Reflected in the night-time window in front of me, I could see eight-year-old "Mick" on the far side of the wide kitchen. "Mick"—no, this week it was "Max"—was slumped against the blond, knotty pine paneling as he perched on the tipped edge of the oak stool near the wall phone. He was sure to fall off and bruise some body part at least twice during this intense conversation with "super-best friend" Guy Schwartz.

Now, I was sure about Guy's name. His family was our nearest neighbor. And it's not that I didn't know the name of my own second son, born a full three minutes before his twin sister, Kit. But just as J.D. tried instruments and interests on for size, "Max" was searching for a new identity. "Max" had dismissed his given name, Benjamin James, as too "boring and old-fashioned." B.J. was out because his brother went by his initials. Benny, Benjie (like the dog!), and any variation of James were "too stupid." Plain Ben was just "too plain."

"Max" was O.K., but somehow it didn't fit this sturdy freckle-faced, red-head with his passionate, imaginative nature. He might look like a pug-nosed brawler, but he was a lover who dreamed of lofty ideals. I had an inkling he dearly wanted to be a knight, but was embarrassed to admit it. Other boys were drawn to his strength and ingenuity. He never lacked for friends. It was his identity within the family that was undergoing a crisis. I think he was trying to define himself as similar to, yet unique from, the big brother he adored and competed against constantly.

"Max . . . Max . . . Max," I practiced under my breath, rinsing the bubbles from the last spoon. I wished he would soon realize how special Ben already is, just the way he is.

"Ow!"

When I turned around, Max said, "It's okay, Mom, just banged my head." He rubbed said body part and continued with the kitten report.

I dried off my chapping hands and moved over to the scrubbed oak counter to cut the cooled honey cake. Every night before bed, we had family devotions, but tonight was dessert n' devotions, a weekly tradition we all looked forward to, each for varying reasons.

Reaching up to pull a knife out of the wall rack, I glanced out the wide picture window over the end of the long plank table already set with place mats and milk glasses. In the back yard, a waning moon broke through the ragged dark clouds, washing the snow-covered humps in the ruined garden with a silvery glow. The warm, golden room scented with cinnamon and ginger reflected in this side of the pane, and the chill, harshly-lit shadows outside mirrored the war within me.

I stood transfixed, the knife heavy in my hand. I was so restless and encumbered. Everywhere I moved were responsibilities, people's needs, and noise. Like Jacob Marley, I had forged ponderous chains—good ones, not evil—but they still had to be dragged with me, eternally, it seemed. I wasn't up to this! I was tired. How could I mother this brood when I didn't know what I was doing? What if I ruined them forever? How could I be the wife Joe deserved when I'd never learned how? Is this all there is?

Yes, God had given me the desires of my heart. But now I seemed to want—to need—something else. How could I be so ungrateful?

This rambling, old, cordial house was full of family, and, so far, by the Lord's grace, full of love. Settled with age, it rests, nestled in a stand of pines, on a hilltop, where the sloping front porch commands a view of the braided green knolls of Waneka Valley. At the end of the valley, towers

Mount Kaniksa, squatting like a brooding hen over her chicks. The first time we drove up the winding gravel road to these eighty acres of hills and tall trees, it felt like home. At least it did to Joe, raised as he was on a farm among the endless, rolling wheatfields of southeastern Washington's Palouse.

Our little Morning Star Farm was a secure, comfortable place with space to grow, but I had begun to feel lifeless and decayed like the frozen winter stalks in the yard.

I laid down the knife, walked around the counter, and pressed my forehead up against the cold glass. (How many times had I told the kids not to do it?) I watched the swift-moving clouds in the windy sky, longing . . . to do something great . . . to wake up in a different place tomorrow. Along with family, I had intended to have a life of valuable, even noble service for God. Why had He narrowed my course to this?

"Race you down the hall, Daddy!" That was Kit, Katherine Gayle, Max's serene and nurturing eight-year-old (minus three minutes) sister. They shared hazelly-brown eyes and lots of secrets, though not so many lately. Kit had my fine, wavy hair that Joe said was like caramel silk.

I had to smile. Of course, Ben/Max came by his romanticism naturally. Along with his charm, Joe's humor and patience made him a beloved pediatrician and an excellent father. But then, he'd grown up in a large, affectionate brood with cheerful Nomi and Bert for parents. I, on the other hand, came from a showy Bel Air mansion headed by a socially ambitious mother and a distant, often-absent father. Neither they, nor my gifted, much older half-brother, Read, had much use for a gawky, inquisitive little girl.

"I want a piggyback ride, Daddy, puhleeze!" I could just imagine our dramatic four-year-old, Lyssa, dimpling at her favorite human being. Alyssa Karisse is the youngest, but she makes up for it with the sheer force of her personality. Born with curling raven hair, violet eyes, and overflowing with self-confidence, she knows in her heart that she can keep up with, or outdo her elder siblings in everything.

Then it occurred to me. If Lyssa was demanding a piggyback, my whole troop would be invading the kitchen any minute. I made myself pull away from the window, and rolled my hunched shoulders. Unkinking my neck, I spotted yet another cobweb undulating overhead in the warm air near the ceiling. Must add whacking it down to my mental *To Do* list.

In the glass, the burnished copper light made dark hollows stare back at me. The shadows fell across my wide mouth which, until recently learned to smile easily and often. Everything was as it should be. Nothing had changed. Why had I?

Irritating beeps cut into my self-absorption. I looked round to see the abandoned telephone receiver dangling by its kinky cord, and banging gently against the scarred, knotted wall.

The marathon of story-telling, tucking, kissing, back-rubbing, whispering, water-drinking, and bedtime praying was finished. I was dragging along on one more sweep through the family room to pick up stray toys, books, and papers. Then there was that one last load of laundry to put in before I went upstairs to collapse in bed myself.

Shakespeare described me well: my sleeve of care was so raveled, I could hardly wait to slip into unconsciousness, hoping tonight there would be some knitting.

Joe was plopped in his roomy plaid recliner in front of the dwindling fire. Though his face was buried in a medical journal, he stuck out his stocking foot and neatly tripped me into his lap, scattering most of my armload. I only sputtered for a minute. Maybe a cuddle wouldn't hurt. I tossed the rest of my gathered booty back on the floor.

"Oh, Joe!" His arms felt good around me. I nuzzled up close to the sandpapery cords of his neck. He smelled faintly of wood smoke and oregano and spicy aftershave.

I was afraid of what *I* smelled, or looked like, after a day like today. My morning beauty routine consisted of the five minutes I took to wash my face and pull my hair back into a tawny ponytail.

"At least close your eyes," I murmured into the collar of his soft flannel shirt.

"Why? You got something to hide?"

Of course, he then pulled back for a thorough examination that ended with raised eyebrows and a charming leer in those marvelous eyes. "As a physician, and a husband, I see nothing wrong with you, Madam, that, say, a little backrub would not cure."

Then, in spite of my looking like something the cat had dragged onto the back step: all frazzled and frumpy in my faded pink sweats and a sloppy pair of his own thick basketball socks; Joseph L. Daniels, Sr., M.D., began to competently stroke my back.

"Eve, you are a beautiful woman no matter what you wear, madeup or not. Sure, you're a knockout when you're all dressed up, but then I hate to touch you for fear of messing you up. You know I like you better all casual and comfortable cause then I can do this . . . ."

He ran his long fingers up my spine, leaned forward and began to kiss my neck. At the same time, he slipped the elastic band out of my hair and combed his fingers through it until it swung out past my shoulders, loose and free.

Is it any wonder I love this guy? In quiet moments when I can focus on him, I am always aware of that enduring and mutual thrill of attraction between us.

Tonight, the care, the tenderness just didn't fit. I didn't feel at all beautiful or loveable with that unhappiness knotted up inside like a twisted wet dishrag. I didn't deserve—nor did I especially want—to be made less unhappy, even momentarily.

"Honey, don't. I can't . . . I'm not . . . just . . . ." Then I surprised us both by bursting into stormy tears. Normally I'm not the hand-wringing, weepy type.

Shocked at this unexpected turn of events, Joe at once transformed into my solicitous, uncomfortable friend.

"What is it, honey?" He patted his pockets for a Kleenex, anything to mop up the flood. "You've been gloomy for days."

"Oh, here!" Just as he discovered a tissue down between the cushions in his chair, the phone began to ring. He waved the crumpled paper under my runny nose. Cross-eyed, I inspected it with suspicion.

"Ignore the phone," he urged. "They can always call back later." We did have an answering machine, but when we were home we almost always forgot to turn it on.

"Couldn't it be your service? An emergency?"

*Ring. Ring.*

"I'm not on call tonight, Ray is."

Joe shares a family practice with three other doctors in the city of Kamas Falls, which starts its modest sprawl about fifteen miles south of our farm.

*Ring. Ring.*

"Well, I can't stand it. I'll get it." I sniffed into the tissue, shoving myself off his lap and out of his reach. My head was pounding, and I was more than a little embarrassed and angry at myself for pushing him away when he had been so attentive.

"I need to get up and go to bed anyway. Joe . . . I . . . I'm sorry about . . . ."

*Ring. Ring.*

"It's okay. I'm sorry you feel so rotten." He bent his tall frame to collect the scattered residue from the floor. "I didn't mean to push you into anything . . . ."

*Ring. Ring.*

I put my hand on the receiver.

"Tell 'em to call back tomorrow. Then we could talk about it, if you want to."

There wasn't really anything to talk to anybody about. If I was already in the center of God's will for my life, He'd give me the strength to survive. I didn't even want to think about being joyful.

I gave my nose one last good blow. "Hello?" Maybe the caller would take a hint from the weary disinterest in my voice.

"Eve? . . . Eve Daniels? Oh, finally! I've been trying and

trying to get through to you. This is Marion Kilmer. Shay's roommate? We met three years ago at your home there in Washington."

There was a strange pitch to the woman's voice that carried across the miles, through the whistling, scratchy connection. Suddenly, my teary preoccupation with self was arrested by a sense of dread.

Of all possibilities as to who the caller might be, Marion Kilmer calling long distance from Morocco had not even figured in the realm of thought. My dearest friend in all the world, Shauna Cathleen O'Shea—known as Shay, "because it's easier for all non-Irish to pronounce,"—teaches high school English and is Marion's partner in an unofficial Bible translation ministry in the ancient cultural center of Fez. Shay calls herself and her teammates "God's secret agents."

"What did you say?" I didn't want to believe what Marion had just blurted out.

"I said, 'I thought you'd want to know, your being such good friends and all, that Shay's been kidnapped.' It appears she's been taken by a Spanish-based terrorist group called the Volcares."

"Why? Never heard of them. What did they take Shay for? Do they want money?" Questions came tumbling out as I tried to shift my brain to the unfriendly reality of an alien world.

"They promote themselves as 'Overthrowers'—the harbingers of a new conservative Islamic order. Publicly, they say they believe that if they help Muslims do away with Western indulgences, the blessing of Allah will come to the Moroccan people.

Shay—a "Western indulgence?"

Marion went on. "But a national security man told us the Volcares' real activities have always been lucrative gun-running, and political agitation. They're backed by communists, Libyans, Algerians—anybody and everybody, it seems."

She gave a weary sigh. "They're just another bunch of quasi-religious bandits who hold people hostage for their own monetary gain.

14

"But, Eve, somehow it's more complicated than a group of terrorists taking a prisoner for ransom. None of us has any money. And we've all been very circumspect in witnessing. Shay was especially careful; yet she was singled out on purpose. They bragged about stalking her for weeks . . . . And . . . . and, that's how they found out about *us*."

Marion's quavery voice tightened down into a precise whisper. I could feel the prickle of goose flesh under my long sleeves.

"They have threatened the rest of us. And their reprisals against enemies are known to be particularly . . . uh, nasty." The nervous woman cleared her throat. "That's why no national wants to cross them, even most of the *Sûreté*. They are afraid for their families."

The words rolled on like it was a relief to share the burden with someone safe and far away. "Shay didn't come home after her late class yesterday evening. Dick, Alex, Robin, and I looked for her most of last night. Then this morning—it's Tuesday here—there was a letter signed by the Volcares stuck to our apartment door with . . . with a bloody knife." She wavered on that last phrase as she relived the horrible moment.

"It made rambling references to their *Jihad*, or holy war. And it went on about our offenses to Allah and the rightful Islamic government."

I could hear Marion beginning to hyperventilate. My own throat was clenching shut in response to the terror that made it difficult for her to continue.

"There were hints of ritual sacrifice . . . of all of us infidel women . . . ."

I strained to hear the bare trace of her speech. "Eve, true Muslim extremists often belong to these political organizations for their own purposes. They'll stop at nothing if they believe killing Shay, and the rest of us, is their necessary—or expedient—religious duty."

A long moment of dead, expensive silence flowed between us.

The muscles in my face didn't seem to respond normally. My lips were so stiff, they wouldn't form words. "What . . . can I do to help?" I finally stammered.

"Well, uh," Marion cleared her throat as if she needed time to think it over. "We . . . need friends to pray for all of us The home board has called all of its prayer chains into action for us anonymously. Maybe you could call your church's prayer warriors to intercede for Shay. It would help to know lots of people are bringing our names before God." Her voice was shaky.

Pray? Sure I'd pray. It was automatic. I had already begun conversing with the Lord in one section of my mind. But, my special, spirited Shay had been stolen by rabid crazies, and all I could do was pray? What did Marion really want from me?

"Isn't anyone out looking for her? Can't you possibly tell the police or Interpol or our embassy . . . somebody?" I wanted action of some kind.

"Eve, you know officially we don't exist. If we call attention to ourselves, even as expatriates with legal work permits, we risk exposing our true occupation." Her tremulous voice was becoming shrill as it rose. "We have enemies who'd jump at any chance to discredit us just because we're Westerners. And there are hundreds like us scattered throughout the Arab world. If certain people found out what we're really doing . . . . Well, the danger of retaliation, for all of us, and innocent foreigners, is just too great."

She paused, facing the import of her next words. Was there a tinge of pride, or regret? "I don't know if Shay told you, but before we could join the group here we had to pledge we'd give our lives, if necessary, to protect the work, or the other team members."

She rushed on as though embarrassed by her dramatic pronouncement. "Actually, Alex does have some acquaintances in different branches of the police force, but local officers can't get involved without high-level cooperation between agencies. And Alex doesn't think that's likely to happen.

"See the Volcares have taken Shay out of the city where the Urban Corps has no jurisdiction. Alex's friend in the Fez police is supposed to be talking to someone he trusts in the *Sûreté Nationale* right now."

I heard a low rumbling, and Marion's aside to someone on her side of the ocean. "Listen, Eve, I have to go now. Thanks for listening and for your prayers. It means a lot to all of us." Marion sounded like she was suddenly forcing herself to be upbeat and perky.

"Wait! Give me a number where I can reach you, or someone who'll know what's going on."

She dictated the home numbers of the two families as well as a work phone. Then the bass rumbling echoed again.

"Thank you very much. Goodbye." Marion hung up.

"What's happened to Shay?" Joe's voice sounded far away, too.

My hand was glued to the phone as though reluctant to break the tiny contact with the friend of my friend who was in deep trouble.

"What is it, Eve? Honey?" Joe demanded again, louder this time. "Has Shay been hurt?"

I managed to look up at my husband, who was actually standing right beside me. His arms were piled high with the children's discards, and under that shock of black hair, concern corrugated his forehead.

I began to move my tongue, but it felt so dry and swollen it choked me. The moisture that belonged in my mouth welled back up into my eyes, and for the second time that night, the collected toys and socks and books were tumbled back on the floor. This time, I stayed in the refuge of Joe's arms.

So stupid! Like some sniveling, Gothic heroine, I just couldn't seem to quit crying tonight.

# 2

Every time I closed my eyes, scenes from the past played behind the lids.

There was Shay, her short carrot curls flying, running down the green slope, "Lyndy! Lyndy! I got it! I got it!"

Christened Eve-Lynn Day Marshall, in order to appease various rich relatives, I grew to hate that affected amalgam of *Lynn* and *Day*—*Lyndy*—stuck on me early by my half-grown brother Read. But my mother loved it. It fit right in with all the *Missys* and *Buffys* and *Jennys* in the other upper class L.A. families.

By the time Shay flung herself and the thick script down on my sunny spot of grass in the quad, she was still squealing and almost speechless in her delight. Almost.

In those college years, if Shay and I had lost the capacity to talk, we would have communicated with hand signals, written notes, or mental telepathy. For the first time in our lives, we each had found someone our own age we could trust with our unvarnished innermost selves. We laughed, debated, and dreamed together incessantly, reveling in our shared acceptance.

I rolled over and opened my eyes. Here was the present. I snuggled back up warm and close to Joe, who had held me until he had fallen into an exhausted sleep. Yesterday had been hard for him, too, and he had another eight o'clock meeting at the hospital—I looked at the bedside clock—later on this morning.

But every time I shut my eyes, what kept coming back was that day Shay ran to tell me she'd won the role of Dulcinea in the Highland University production of "Man of La Mancha."

I'd bullied her to try out for the part in spite of her terror at all the memorization and the solos required. I'd also had to vow to help her learn her lines and work some of her cafeteria hours for her. That's what we did for each other—acted as cheerleader, or confidant, or conscience.

Shauna Cathleen O'Shea was a short pixie with a redhead's creamy skin and jade green eyes. However, taking after her tough, hard-living, and quick-fisted father, Sean, a crane operator on the Long Beach docks, Shay wasn't as fragile as she looked.

The only daughter among four sons, Shay grew up in a rough home on a mean street near the harbor. By the age of twelve, she could fight dirty and drink hard with the rest of the "dock brats."

She attacked life with great bursts of frenetic energy, and would often collapse into sleep at a moment's notice. The effort of keeping her two selves integrated, demanded this constant payment. Because even in those years near the docks, this swearing, swinging spitfire had the gentle, star-lit soul of a poet.

Shay set her sights on a college education. Her dream was to be a teacher. She worked her way through Long Beach Junior College, where she also became an enthusiastic Christian through a campus ministry. Then she hurled herself at Highland.

Though unable to help financially, and scornful of her new "religious" lifestyle; her dad, her weary mother, and even most of her rowdy brothers were already bragging about the first college-educated O'Shea. She scraped by on faith, brains, a combination of obscure scholarships, loans, and work-study.

"The Lord pulled strings to get me here," she'd say, "now with His help I'm going to make Him proud." So she worked incessantly, made high grades, and rejoiced in every moment spent with the lyrical wonder of Shakespeare, the emotion of Herbert, or the biting humor of Twain.

She was so focused. I, on the other hand, was a haphazard drifter, searching for purpose. "We're so different. I don't know how we get along so well," I'd muse.

"Well, we're opposites of the same kind," was my friend's reply.

Shay was right. We were opposites. I was much too tall to be mistaken for a sprite. And even though slender, I was strong and tanned from the years of helping Serafina with her hardest chores, from competing in the barrio's boisterous street games, and from joining in the outdoor pastimes of the wealthy.

If anyone looked past my deliberate gray eyes, and quiet demeanor, within they would have seen a restless, even unruly soul: domesticated, but not fully tamed. I craved action, not just beautiful words. As a young college sophomore of barely eighteen, I hadn't even identified an educational goal. I appeared to be a golden child floating through life on wealth and privilege.

Shay was right. We were the same kind. I, too, lived a dual life.

By the time I was eight or nine, the succession of my ineffectual nannies ended. Frustrated with the constant interruption of her schedules by distraught or unreliable employees, mother basically left me to my own devices. I was a wild child until Serafina intervened.

Serafina was our housekeeper and my salvation. A widow with seven children, but enough love for seventy, "*Tia* Sera" took over the job of raising me. As long as the Bel Air neighbors never knew, and as long as I was polished up and available for trips or civic functions where a daughter was an asset to the image, Elaina Lynn Marshall, my biological mother, expediently chose to ignore my relationship with Sera.

Informally adopted, I was often taken into Sera's home, and tacked on as the last of *mi Tía's* brood like a changling child or an ugly duckling. Carlos, Pablo, Jorge, and Tomas, her almost grown sons, cuffed me and teased me and protected me from their own unkind or dangerous neighbors like four young fathers. Sera's daughters, Ana, Teresa, and Rebeca, in their teens and twenties, became my sisters.

So the daughter of the successful international lawyer, Maston Read Marshall, really grew up in Van Nuys. *Tía* Sera nurtured, and civilized, and led me to salvation through Jesus Christ in the Valley's Hispanic community that lies in the shadow of some of the earth's priciest real estate—my supposed home. My true home was with Sera and her family. They were faithful Christians who taught me the meaning of love.

The trips to Cannes or Rome with my socialite mother; and our rare, required meetings in Geneva or London with my formal father seemed like punishments to me. Any time spent alone in the cavernous house on the hill, or at the rich kids' schools I attended, was wasted, unreal, pointless. Real life for me had been lived at the bottom of the hills in a hot, smoggy valley.

"I can't believe it. *I'm* Dulcinea! Oh, Lyndy, help me start learning my lines. Please?" My dream about Shay came back.

"Right now?"

"Oh, yes! I've got so much to learn. This way you can kind of be in it with me."

She rolled over on her stomach and opened the script where we both could see.

"It's too bad I can't sing bass. I'd make a great Don Quixote. I've been tilting at windmills all my life." I said.

"You've got a great voice. Why do you think I first wrangled a seat next to you in choir? Hmmm . . . maybe we could talk old Potts into making this an all-female production."

"You bet," I laughed. Let's start here."

With round tones, I read aloud the first words of the noble, delusional hero:

Hear me now, oh thou bleak and unbearable world!
Thou art base and debauched as can be;
And a knight with his banners unfurled
Now hurls down his ("No, her!") gauntlet to thee!

In between giggles, Shay sat up and joined me loudly in song:

I am I, Don Quixote,
The Lord of La Mancha,
My destiny calls and I go;
And the wild winds of fortune will carry me onward,
Oh whithersoever they blow.

Whithersoever they blow,
Onward to glory I go!

People in the quad turned to stare, but we didn't care.

## 3

A t five-thirty, I slid out of the useless bed and splashed my face with cold water. I was sure what I needed—wanted—to do, but not how to go about it.

Addressing my crow's feet in the small mirror, I mocked, "You're getting old and lazy, complacent and scared—all those things you were *never* going to be!"

Scrubbing with soap to scour away the gray sleeplessness, I mentally continued my lecture. "You haven't been stuck. Nobody's 'held you down.' It's been your own choice to stay put here with a husband and family responsibilities."

I tied the fuzzy apricot robe over my red flannel nightgown. Then I put on the huge Mickey Mouse slippers the kids had given me at Christmas. "Are you up to new challenges again, old girl?"

In my oversized footwear, I scuffled down the cold hall past the kids' rooms. I peeked in on Kit and Lyssa in their twin beds looking angelic and cozy. They still enjoyed sharing a room—most of the time. Ben, in his room next door, had kicked the quilt to the floor, and was sprawled face-down across the old double bed. No one could sleep with him. Not only did he thrash around, he also yelled out loudly at intervals all night long. I scuffed in and re-covered him with the quilt. He always slept soundly, even when he prevented anyone else near him from doing so.

I looked at the lighted dial on Ben's clock. Good. There was still time before the mad rush for breakfast and the bus. I was often grateful that the bus stopped right at the end of our long driveway!

As usual, J.D.'s light was visible from the basement stairway as I reached the dark living room. His internal alarm went off early every morning to allow him time for reading or other projects.

I made sure my kids could choose between pleasurable solitude or companionship. But I still found myself amazed at how much we all honestly enjoyed each another's company. My childhood dream of a family had come true, so why couldn't I be content?

I put the kettle on to boil, then retrieved my big, tattered Bible from the dusty top of the refrigerator. It smacked when I dropped it on the kitchen table and stepped over to push aside the shutters, anticipating the icy, bright beginning of a clear January day.

The anxieties of the night had given way to a strong sense of direction and purpose. I realized I was actually humming under my breath. So I watched for the sun. I talked some more with God, and I listened.

Before anyone else really began to stir, I was on my way back upstairs with two white mugs of pungent spice tea. I kicked at our bedroom door with my well-padded foot, this time waking Tandy, our arthritic old shepherd who sleeps curled up on the braided rug at the foot of the king-sized bed. She greeted me with dim eyes and a *thump-thump* of her stubby tail.

"Go back to sleep, girl." I said in a stage whisper. "It's your dad I want to wake up."

Perching nearly on top of him, since his lanky frame occupied a large portion of even a king-size bed, I was half-anchored to a small slice of leftover mattress edge. "Good morning, handsome," I cooed. "Could I interest you in something hot?"

One of Joe's eyes opened wide and looked me up and down.

"Just what is it that you are offering me this morning, Madam?" He grinned and opened the other eye. Joe doesn't require a lot of sleep to recharge his batteries. I guess he learned that during internship.

"You're asking that of a haggard woman in Mickey Mouse slippers?"

"I told you last night, it's not the wrapping, it's what's inside that counts."

I stuck the mug under his nose. "*This* is what I had in mind, along with a little conversation. After all, it is a school morning and you have an eight o'clock meeting all the way downtown at St. Cami's."

"Fine, we've already had a little conversation. The kids start their own breakfast, the lunches are in the fridge, and I don't care if I'm late to this review. Put the mug down . . . ."

So I did.

Miraculously, we didn't even run too far behind schedule. As the kids cleaned up their dishes and loaded their backpacks, I went back upstairs with some hot tea to corner Joe while he shaved and shrugged into work clothes: a pullover sweater and jeans.

"I might as well be comfortable," he'd say. "Studies show that ties and tight collars cut off blood flow to the brain. People don't need a fancy dresser, they need a smart doctor."

Kamas Falls wasn't a small town, but it still had a casual country feel, so he fit right in. Besides, he was a great doctor, and looked better in jeans than a lot of men look in a tux.

"I want to fly to Morocco to help find Shay," I blurted out. Before he could contradict me, I pushed on. "I don't want to kill off what we've managed to save, so I thought I'd take money out of one of the funds. Neither has ever been closed, you know."

Joe, who had sat down on the bed beside me, stopped in the process of pulling on his boot, and stared at me in disbelief.

"I *know* what I've always said about using any of that money. But, if there was ever an emergency, this is it. And I think it fits the legal conditions. Joe, I've prayed and thought about it all night. It's not like I'd be taking it to support us or myself or buy goodies. Maybe this is the very reason God gave me rich grandparents, and my father couldn't break the will, and my mother has never been able to touch it either." I gulped, pausing for a much-needed breath.

"Honey . . . ," he began.

I jumped in before he could continue. "I need to be there, Joe, to actually do something to try and get her back. Something besides praying and phone calls . . . . I, well, I used to know my way around Morocco pretty well . . . ." I finished lamely.

Joe had risen to face me. He stood there huge and silent. His black brows were knitted.

"I . . . ," I started to bargain.

"No, don't do that," he said quietly, taking my hands in his.

"Don't go?" Hot anger flared in me; I jerked away from him. "You have no right! I can do this without you if I have to."

He held up his hands like a policeman halting traffic. "Whoa! Before you let that temper loose, I meant you don't have to wheedle or convince or..." he pinned my eyes with a steady stare, "bully me, Eve. I agree. I think you *should* go to Morocco to be closer to Shay. I'm only concerned about your safety. And, since you'll probably be hanging around with the police, I can't see how you'd be in any danger. What's happened sounds like more of a vendetta against Shay herself.

Marion had said they'd all been threatened. I'm sure I told

26

him that. But he'd evidently thought it through. So, he had to be right. As an outsider, virtually a tourist, I would be in no danger.

"You *do* know the country after your trips with the mobile medical teams, and you still keep in contact with the guy who works for that Moroccan godfather." Joe continued. Then he frowned, "Of course, he may be personal friends with the terrorists."

I bounced straight up into his strong embrace. "Oh, Joe, no wonder I love you!" I muttered against his chest.

His lips were close to my ear. "I'm glad you are going to use the money for this. It's like lancing something that's been festering far too long. This redeems it . . . gives it new meaning."

"I never thought I would say this, but for the first time I'm actually glad both grandmothers left the trusts to me with the stipulation that they be used only for personal pleasure. Nothing could give me more pleasure than finding Shay."

He let go, and bent back to the job of pulling on his boots. "Don't take this the wrong way, honey," he said with his eyes on his feet, "you know how I feel about Shay, but, it'll be good for you to get away from the routine around here for a while, too. You've been getting wound up tighter and tighter, till I've been afraid you'll break."

Joe stood up and fixed me with that impelling gaze. "The kids and I will do okay for awhile without you . . . but not forever."

He stooped down and gave me a sweet peck on the forehead. "Give Gina a call about watching the kids after school. I'll call you later and we'll talk some more."

Then, before I could respond, he was out the door and down the stairs. I could hear him rounding up the three older children, shooing them out the back door for the bus as he left. I didn't get to kiss them goodbye, but Lyssa and I waved to them from the bedroom window.

# 4

The high puffy columns of cloud were dazzling against the intensely blue sky. Floating lazily above the earth, surrounded by heaven's light and color was my favorite part of flying. In fact, I loved all the results of boarding a plane. But this morning, I was almost too exhausted, too numb to care. My brain felt as fluffy and insubstantial as my cloudy companions.

I'd reached the last leg of a very long journey, quickly conceived and hastily undertaken. This was the first time in . . . how long had we been married?. . . in twelve years that I had ventured this far from home and loved ones alone. I missed Joe and the children. I feared what might be happening to Shay. But I was undeniably exhilarated over my solo expedition.

Marion's call had come Tuesday night. After Joe and the kids left on Wednesday morning, the first person I called was dusty old Richard Bayley of Bayley, Pritchard, Reynolds and Bayley. The lawyer had seemed incredibly withered and ancient when I used to see him in our Bel Air house as a child. But mummification suited him, evidently, for he was still the Bayley running the firm. After all these years, I had expected to have to do my business with his slimy son, Forrest.

Forrest Bayley, just a little older than I, was as oily as his father was dehydrated. At social gatherings, I had always made an effort to never find myself alone with him. The one and only time he succeeded in cutting me out of the herd, Forrest had gone home with a set of well-placed bruises. But that had never caused him to quit trying.

"So, Lyndy Marshall," the elder Bayley wheezed over the phone. "You've finally come begging. Glad I lived to see it. That cult you join finally drop you flat? Or is it the husband?

"Remember, my dear, you can't use the trust monies to support your own family, nor any religious or non-profit agencies. You'll have to submit proof to me of any and all planned disbursements."

The wave of nausea that hit me at the sound of his voice was almost overwhelming. I thought I could do this, but it was like opening a grave.

*Help me, Lord. This is for Shay. Give me the right words to say, please.* I prayed silently and tried to still my shaking hands.

"Mr. Bayley, I go by my legal first name now—Eve. And my married name is Daniels." The voice coming out of my mouth sounded polite and confident. Good idea to mention anything legal. Mr. Bayley loved every jot and tittle of man-made law.

"I wish to withdraw some funds for myself in order to take a trip to Morocco." I couldn't believe I was actually saying this. It had taken a long time, and a desperate situation.

At nineteen, in my junior year, it being the 'in' thing to do, I was sent around the world to take a semester of classes on the shipboard branch of my university, the S.S. WorldFind. Removed to the farthest reaches of ocean, and unprepared to face the shocking human deprivation and misery on other continents, I reached out to the Lord in new ways. In those few months, my faith deepened, I found a purpose and my life was transformed. There was a world of hurt out there, and I wanted to be used by the Savior to help bring healing to it. In each port of call, I visited missions, hospitals, churches and received a real education.

Instead of returning home at the end of that semester, I jumped ship in Japan and linked up with Ship of Hope, a missionary vessel that sails among the neediest places on the globe and provides major medical assistance along with the Gospel.

Starting as only an untrained but willing pair of extra hands, they took me on. I thought I had done mucky work alongside *Tía* Sera, but I hadn't imagined anything remotely close to some of the things I eventually learned to do on the good ship Hope. In the quick and dirty world of "bush" medicine, I discovered I was far stronger and more useful than I had ever been in my life.

Reluctantly, I came home late in the summer before my twentieth birthday—at Mother's insistence. All members of the Day and Marshall clans were required to come back from wherever in the world they happened to be in time to make an appearance at Mamaw Day's ninetieth birthday party.

"After all, love, you don't want to be the one to cause *su mama* any more public embarrassment in the society section of the *Times*, now do you, darling? You've *always* chosen to run with such low class people, and go to such *revolting* places." It had been one of her less threatening long distance suasions.

Once I'd agreed to come back to the States, I began to plan the quickest way to obtain a degree in nursing—it wouldn't take as long as getting an M.D.—and get back to the ship for as long as the Lord could use me.

The Lord had other plans.

The family that had paid me so little heed for so long immediately rallied against "my foolishness." Instead of sniping at each other, they found they could unite heartily against me.

Certainly, I could go into medicine, they agreed.

"Look at brother Read, now a microbiologist making quite a name for himself in scientific circles."

But I must choose something sane, and lucrative like psychiatry or surgery. "Study something one practices at the most prestigious hospitals," Grandmother Marshall sniffed.

As for the weird religious idealogies such as predicting who was going to heaven and who was not, I'd gone too far! They decided it had all started with that crazy Serafina. She should have never been allowed to fill my mind with such emotional tripe. "But she was so *sneaky* about it," mother protested to the others.

*Now* they conceded, one *should* try to be a good person and do his or her best and give money to charity every year. But I could really *be* somebody. To throw that all away for a life cleaning up "the overpopulation of sick and dirty savages," well, that would be worse than foolish.

I was officially forbidden to entertain such thoughts any longer. I was ordered not to see Sera or her family, or write to my shipboard friends.

I was also never to have contact with "that young fellow . . . what was his name?" that I'd met when he'd served a short term on board ship. "He's just a poor farm boy," they said, "who wants to get his hands on your money so he can finish his medical training and set up a cushy practice."

Ah, money! And the accumulation of piles of it, was the favorite topic for my relatives that weekend. Money is, after all, power.

Grandmothers Day and Marshall, who'd set up large trusts for Read and myself, put their heads together. On Monday, at Mr. Bayley's decorous offices, my considerable accounts, available to me after my twenty-fifth birthday, were reorganized with new stipulations.

When I came of age, I would only be able to use the money for personal benefit. Excluded were gifts to charitable organizations (particularly religious ones). And no money could be given to any future husband or children

I might someday acquire.

The money didn't matter to me. God would provide. But how could I survive without the work that my heart longed for, or the people who'd filled my life with love?

I knew I was supposed to honor my parents, but I also wanted to honor God. Attempting to be mature and not run off mad to follow my own desires, I prayed, fasted, and unsuccessfully tried to plead my case the rest of that August.

Thank the Lord, I hadn't been forbidden to see Shay or Pastor Ruiz from my home church in Van Nuys. Shay was a college friend, which, presumably, made her still tolerable. (No family member had ever talked to her long enough to find out what she was *really* like—or where she came from.) And, it was beyond their imagining, that I would be a member of a barrio church, much less call a—well, a minority person—my minister.

Pastor and Shay contacted those I wasn't permitted to get in touch with and they, in turn, all prayed with me for an answer.

Come September, I was due back at Highland, where it was time to declare a major. I also knew what I had to do.

"Mother, I need to talk to you." I'd been trying for days to get an appointment with her. When she rushed in from an afternoon at the Club, I followed her into her room and waited, working at being patient while she showered. When the water stopped, I knocked on the locked door.

"Not now, Lyndy. I'm having dinner with the mayor, and I'm already late." She came bursting out of the inner bathroom door, her expensively coiffed hair and age-defying body wrapped in velvety white towels. She headed straight for the room-sized closet. "And I don't appreciate your barging in here. You know I like my privacy," she commented over her shoulder.

My mother emerged from the clothes room with four different outfits draped over her arms. "We can have a talk some other time," she said, separating a royal blue silk pantsuit for closer consideration. "Actually, I can't think of anything else that need be said right now."

Father must have thought that, too. He left for Bonn two days after Mamaw's party. He never even said goodbye.

"Mother, fall semester starts at Highland day after tomorrow. A decision has to be made."

She was laying her chiffon-and-beaded choices carefully on top of the massive white satin bedspread. Her mind was on the color scheme for tonight's banquet.

"I'm willing to cut off the relationships you want if you really believe they're bad for me. But I'm convinced God's called me to get nurse's training and serve Him overseas somehow. If not on that ship, then in some way. So I still really want to study nursing." I said it all in one breath, sensing I had to get it out quickly. I didn't have much experience telling my mother what I felt.

She regarded me sideways a moment, still fondling a silver-sequined sheath. The bright lights of the makeup mirror made those sequins shimmer and dance as they flowed over her hands. Twisting her head, she impaled me with her cool gray eyes.

"Very well, dear, since you insist, we'll get our necessary little chat over with here and now. It won't take long."

Mother turned her back and draped the sheath across the delicate Louis XIV brocade chair. Then she whirled back around, and faced me directly. It was the first and last time she spoke right at me.

"To tell you the truth, Lyndy, I don't really much care what you or your God wants. Your father has left me for good this time. And I won't be able to afford to support you on the allowance he is giving me, even with my inheritance. So, I guess you can pretty much do whatever you want. You'll get your own money in five years."

The effort of communicating with me was unbearable. Mother turned back to study her beautiful face in the glaring mirror. She tapped lightly at her throat with the backs of her fingers.

"But I warn you, it won't be enough to live on." Extending

33

her neck forward like that made her teeth clench. "With all your wonderful friends, I'm sure you'll get by. Maybe nurse's training is a good idea after all. At least you can always find some kind of job when the romance of sacrifice wears off."

There had been so much information thrown at me so quickly, I couldn't process it all. "Father's . . . divorcing you?" I stammered. "I . . . I'm sorry."

My family wasn't ideal, but it's still a shock when life as you've known it crumbles in seconds.

My mother pushed away from the looking glass and made a point of picking up her glittering dress. Avoiding my eyes, she laid the chosen sheath apart from the others on the bed. Striding back to the dressing table, she remarked, "Maybe I'm divorcing him . . . your . . . 'father'!" Mother spat the title out with a sneer.

Dismissing that subject, she picked up a jar of French face cream. "You can stay until the end of the week, then I'm closing up the house." She sat down in front of her mirror, and flipped on the radio. Loud. She never looked at me again.

"Mommy, are you sick?" Lyssa, her head cocked to one side was peering at me with a scowl. "Your face looks funny," she pronounced.

"I got a little nervous talking to the man on the phone. He made me remember something sad. I'll be okay," I said in a shaky voice. "Thanks for caring, sweetie." I tried to smile and reached out to touch her soft cheek.

"Can I go get you a glass of water by myself?"

"That would be very nice, Lyssa."

As she bounded off on her errand of mercy, I shook my head to rid it of the aftereffects of Mr. Bayley's inquisition. In spite of his distrusting nastiness, my request passed the test. The money was on its way.

"What can man do to me?" I reassured myself. Then, with rebounding confidence, I dialed Gina Schwartz, Guy's mom.

The Schwartz family lives a half-mile east of us, past the

next turn in the gravel road. Gina, who's thirty-four like me, is an Italian earthmother. Her husband, Nathan, is a mathematics professor and an incurable practical joker. They bought the ramshackle old Parsons' place when the crotchety, widowed farmer gave in to his children and retired to a sunny city apartment.

Gina, a plump, dark beauty with strong arms and equally strong character, is the back-to-the-lander who makes all the repairs to the sagging homestead. She is the modern pioneer woman who grows and puts up all her own food, makes her family's clothes, keeps a herd of goats, and chops the firewood.

All those skills come in handy, for Nathan is a pudgy, Brooklyn cherub with a head for abstract algebra, and a fondness for wicked puns and questionable limericks. (Thankfully, he *is* diligent to reserve the latter for adult company. Whether the adults consent or not, is another matter.)

Dr. Schwartz displays no mechanical or gardening skills whatever. Rather, as an instructor at Brendford College, he carpools back to "semi-civilization" each weekday to teach differential calculus and some other things I'll never understand. Out here in "the wilderness," Nathan is a fish out of water. "As out of place as lox on a sourdough flapjack," is how he puts it.

But both Gina and Nathan agree they want to raise their kids away from the big city. Native New Yorkers, they met and married during graduate school at N.Y.U.

Gina hadn't quite finished her masters when Antonio (Tony) came along, promptly followed by Fredrico (Rico), Angelina (Angie), Guiseppe (Guy), Rosina (Rosie), and Samuele (Sammy).

"I shall continue my book studies someday, Eva," she would say with her incurable need to give my name the lilt of two syllables. "But in the meantime, my *bambinos* teach me about life." Sometimes she was more Italian than others.

"Oh, Eva, please let me watch your little ones," Gina said as soon as I had explained Shay's situation. She always did go right to the heart of a matter.

"They can move in here with us for as long as you want. Then Joseph would have no worries." Of course, sometimes she insisted on doing a triple bypass when chicken soup would do.

"Thanks, Gina—but, nine kids under one roof? In the winter when they don't stay out long?"

"Ah, there will be plenty of us to cuddle together for warmth."

"No, Gina that's not really necessary. Joe can get them off to school and be home by four or five most days for a week or so. The other docs owe him that much coverage already. Besides, you know him, he'd miss them all too much if they were at your house."

"Well, he can . . . ."

"Basically," I cut in before she had permanently adopted every member of my family, "the kids would only need to come to your house after school until Joe gets home. All except Lyssa . . . ."

"What about me, Mommy?" The lady in question came over, sloshing water across the floor out of what must have been the largest glass in the entire kitchen. Lyssa proudly crawled into my now damp lap with her gift.

After wrangling about whether my delighted daughter should spend all the days with Gina and her two youngest, and about Gina's feeding everybody day and night, my generous neighbor reluctantly agreed to my terms. I knew Joe would have to continue to fight off her escalating kindnesses.

"Eva," she promised, "I will light a candle—no two—one for you and one for your friend. And I will pray for you every day you are gone."


"Would Madam like a pillow or a blanket?"

Heart pounding, I jumped at the French-accented question, then struggled to focus on the lovely stewardess' smiling

36

black eyes. Such a polite way of telling me that my head had been lolled forward, and my jaw had sagged open. Ever so casually, I tried wiping my chin with the back of my hand.

At my query, she informed me that it was now Saturday morning, 6:30 a.m., Paris time. The Royal Air Maroc 727 had been in flight for about an hour.

"It will be about one more hour to Fez. Plenty of time for a nice nap with a comfortable pillow," the stewardess assured me as she reached into the compartment overhead and retrieved a small pillow. As she handed it to me, her amused eyes rested on the ragged pink teddy bear I was clutching in my arms.

"Yes, thank you, a nap would be very nice," I said, striving to regain some dignity.

I pulled the shade down and once my head was properly cradled in the corner with Ted Bear and my cramped legs were stretched out over the three seats in my row—this early morning flight was fairly empty—I tried to float back toward real sleep. But my dreams and the sudden wakening had stirred up more than my heart rate. Thoughts of people kept racing around my mind like caged hamsters on a squeaky wheel.

Would J.D. be able to walk to his orthodontist appointment on Monday if it kept snowing? Would anyone remind him to go?

Lyssa might forget me altogether and refuse to come home once she got daily access to Angie and Rosie's amazing doll collection.

And Ben. His last math facts test was coming up next week. He could be the first out of both second grade classes to finish his 20's. Would Joe remember to help him with his drills? Ben wanted so badly to be the first one done.

How many name changes would he undergo while I was gone? Oh, Ben, why can't you just be satisfied being exactly who you are?

My drooping eyelids snapped open. My head reeled as I sat up abruptly.

Why couldn't I?

Maybe Ben had caught his dissatisfaction from me. Hadn't I been longing to redefine myself—again? To be someone else—lately?

Ben was sensitive to feelings. He and I were a lot alike. Maybe that's why his naming project irked me. Maybe *my* discontent irritated my Father.

"Ladies and gentlemen, please fasten your seatbelts. Estimated time of arrival in Fez is seventeen minutes. Thank you."

"*Mesdames et Messieu . . . .*" As the announcement was repeated in French and Arabic, a flash of pink on the floor caught my eye. I had dropped poor Ted.

It was Kit who had thrust her well-loved bear into my arms with the last hugs at the airport Thursday night.

"He'll watch over you and keep you company, Mom." Kit said in her grown-up voice. I could see she fully intended to mother everyone in my absence, or at least boss them around.

"Honey, I can't take your Teddy. He means so much to you."

"You know I don't sleep with him anymore, Mom. But he's still a good friend. I want you to take him. Besides," she added with a knowing smile, "he loves to ride on planes."

Pushing up the window shade, I peered out for my first glimpse of North Africa since—well, a lifetime ago.

I recalled my initial look at Africa as that long ago girl. Casablanca was the WorldFind's first port of call. After days of rough sailing over winter Atlantic swells, a thread on the horizon began to grow into the coast of Morocco. Every passenger, student and teacher, ran to the starboard side of the ship to watch it develop into solid land.

To my astonishment, that shoreline, under chilly gray skies, sprouted the white skyscrapers of a bustling modern city beyond the waterfront. This was Africa, but there were no chanting black natives with spears and thatched huts waiting to greet us to the beat of skin drums. We finally pulled into a misty, European-looking harbor where the cold waves almost toppled the unbalanced ship before we could slip into a berth alongside the dock.

That was January, too. I had been searching for something then. Unexpected finds on that trip—the growth in my walk with the Lord, learning about my true self and talents, even, eventually meeting Joe because of it—had changed my life forever.

I could only pray my search for Shay would be as fruitful.

# 5

With my knees under my chin, I was packed into the back seat of Shay's yellow '62 VW bug. It was a good thing that even after four babies, I hadn't spread sideways—too much—because I had to share the cramped space with two boxes and a pile of rolled bandages.

It was my own fault if I was uncomfortable—physically, that is—because I had insisted on climbing in the back. But I had little control over the social climate inside the car which seemed as frosty as the outside temperature on this winter morning in Fez. More was being restrained in here than just my legs.

After the first rush of standard greetings at the airport, Dick Foster, now grimly silent behind the steering wheel, and Marion, riding stiffly beside him as we shimmied down the highway towards the city, both acted ill-at-ease and not particularly glad to see me.

A muscle twitched in the stocky man's jaw, where he was grinding his back teeth. Marion, a pinched, bony woman, surreptitiously gnawed at the stubby remnants of fingernails.

40

I shouldn't take their silence personally, I thought. They had been in the middle of a frightening situation for nearly a week. But just four days ago, Marion sounded thrilled when I called about my plans to come.

Left alone with my own thoughts, I stared out the blunt oval window at the foreign, yet vaguely familiar sights flying by. When we sputtered past the junction to Khemisset, a place that had touched both of our lives at different times, my memory spun back to the beginning of Shay's love affair with Morocco.

After graduating from Highland, teaching certificate in hand, Shay was willing to take any job she could find. In that era of education in California, the only openings available to new teachers were in the toughest inner-city schools or in the most remote small towns.

My friend, tiny but determined, braved the war zones in several rough city high schools as a substitute teacher. Being a sub anywhere makes you a target of students' contempt, if not their crimes. But being the only very caucasian lady within miles who was struggling to explain the beauty of lyric poetry to gangs of large, hostile young men was— well . . . Shay ended her first year with a bleeding ulcer.

"They need so much more than I can give them," she'd told me over and over again for three full years.

Supporting herself as a waitress, Shay had gone back to school to do graduate work in reading and special education. She was set on reaching those hard cases.

While there, a whole new opportunity opened to her. At State, Shay met Alice Nelson, a teacher at a Moroccan school for the handicapped run by U.S.-based Save the Children. With government sanctions, Horm School in Khemisset provided full-time care and education for disabled children brought from every area of the nation. Not many handicapped Moroccans got such opportunities, so it was a revered institution. Back in the seventies, I'd had a chance to work there briefly as part of the Ship of Hope crew. I knew it was a great place.

Through Alice, Shay was introduced to Dick and Treva Foster, who were also back in the States on 'vacation.' They were completing more credits in linguistics and cross-cultural communications to improve their ministry as Evancroft translators.

The Fosters and their two teenage daughters had no formal ties nor support from the mission because "professional" Christian missionaries are barred from making a home in Morocco. Most Muslim countries have laws prohibiting Christian evangelism.

So, barrel-chested Dick, a strong man with massive hairy forearms, learned leatherworking from local craftsmen. He'd now spent nearly two decades with them in the hot, fetid tannery quarters by the *Oued,* or River, Fez in Morocco's largest *medina.* There, Dick had gained the tolerance and even the grudging respect of some of the least socially mobile members of Moroccan society. Though greatly respected for their world-renowned skill, tanners are rather odoriferous to invite home for dinner.

As though reading my mind, Dick suddenly rolled down the front window. They'd all been shut tight against the morning's cold air. But now sunlight was skipping along the snow-capped ridge of *Djebel Bou Iblane,* the highest peak in the Middle Atlas range, where it rambled south of the city. Golden rays gleamed on the frozen hills closer to Fez, and sunbeams bounced around the polished glass downtown.

Dick could have been opening his window to let in some heat.

"Sorry, Mrs. Daniels. I can't smell it— or much else—anymore, but I know I stink pretty bad." His face softened with an apologetic grin. "I hope you won't be too cold."

"The air feels—and smells good—thanks. And call me Eve, please."

He bobbed his head in acknowledgment. "Eve. Please call me Dick." His eyes told me he wasn't normally a gruff man, just a shy, and, at the moment, a very worried one.

I'd been given a glimpse of the dedicated man who, along

with his vivacious wife, had had such a profound effect on my friend.

After meeting Dick and Treva, Shay began to wonder if God would open a Moroccan ministry for her. While praying with them, with friends at her church, and with me (over the phone), Shay recognized a growing desire to serve with the linguists in Fez.

Since her favorite saying was, "The Lord can't drive a parked car," Shay approached Alice Nelson, who enthusiastically invited her to join the Horm school staff as an English teacher. That was my friend's entree to the country and her open door from the Lord.

It had now been eleven years since Shay, tattered Arabic workbooks in hand, flew off with Alice to what the North Africans call "*El Maghreb el Aksa*": "The Land of the Setting Sun" or "The Land Farthest West." Over time, through her friendship with the small group of "tentmaker" evangelists living in Fez, Shay's talent for capturing God's Word in other languages became known.

Shay met Marion, a Peace Corps volunteer from Iowa, when she took some first aid training at the hospital in Fez. "For my special kids at Khemisset," she wrote. Shay drew the nurse into translation work and the two women began to compile word lists for the book of John in the Berber dialect of the Guerouane tribe.

Four years back, Shay moved from Khemisset to share an apartment with Marion, and a Moroccan Christian nurse, Zubaida, in Fez-*Jedid*, the relatively "newer" portion of the ancient city. While Shay still drove out to Horm school twice a week, she also devoted at least a third of her time to work with Zubaida and Marion, the Fosters, Alex Dawson-Rhys and his wife, Marguerite, translating, composing, editing, doing layout, and even printing materials.

Year before last, Shay had been invited to teach English classes at a private secondary school in the new city. "This way," she had written, "I can work with the young people in every strata of Moroccan society, both rural and city." She was very happy.

"Remember our *Lalla* Fatima?" Marion's voice startled me when she shouted over the grind of the bug's motor.

I scrunched forward to look up to the northwest through the windshield, past the highway filled with traffic. There over the ramparts of aged Fez-*el-Bali* was the bulky hump of Djebel Zalagh. From certain viewpoints, the mountain's silhouette *does* look like a lady lying down.

I remember one of Shay's first letters describing "Lady Fatima," or Mt. Zalagh, and the panoramic view of centuries-old Fez-*el-Bali* as seen from the ancient dynastic tombs resting high up on the slopes of the surrounding hills. "As the tan walls and the green and white roofs turn rose-colored in the setting sun, the *muezzins* cry out from the many minarets to the faithful," she wrote. In my mind's eye, I could see the dusk settle over medieval fountains, mosques, and palaces.

"North Africa is called the *Maghreb* here. That is, the 'Land of the Setting Sun.' I'm in North Africa to serve the living Son!

"Then I found out today," her words flowed on, "that '*Maghreb*' actually came from the Arabic '*gharib*,' which means, 'to go into the unknown.' Those first Arab invaders from the East came here into the unknown carrying their religion with them. So now I come here, too, into the unknown carrying The Words of Life. Eve, *this* is the true *jihad*."


The VW shot off Avenue Hassan II, an imposing boulevard separated by broad beds of trees, and seasonal flowers, into the roundabout encircling the *Place de la Resistance*. Much of the traffic continued around and downhill toward the medina where *Souk-el-Sebt*, the Saturday market, would be in full swing. Dick, however, doubled back, and turned off toward *Ville Nouvelle*, the crowded mass of multi-storied concrete towers where Marion, Zubaida, and Shay lived.

A parking spot opened ahead in the solid line of cars

parked on both sides of *Rue el Inan* when a rusty red Saab shot away from the curb.

"Thank you, Lord," Dick said simply. "And only a block and a half from your building!" He smiled at Marion.

"We all make it a habit to pray for a parking place in this city," Marion tittered a little as Dick lifted my small tote out of the Volkswagen's front trunk.

"God always cares for us in even that small way," Dick added.

I confessed that I pray for a parking place when I go into downtown Kamas Falls. "Sometimes, I've felt selfish or silly to ask for something like that. But His kindness and help in the little hassles of everyday life end up being so . . . comforting, I guess. They help me cope."

"Not many of us are called to be glorious martyrs for our faith, Eve, or to be heroes in world-changing, grand events," Dick said with another grin as he lumbered down the sidewalk beside me toward building 303. "But we can all honor Him in the small happenings of our mundane, daily routines."

Dick, a "secret agent" for the Lord, living in an exotic foreign country, had to put up with boring day-to-day routines? Why do I forget that into *every* life a little tedium will fall?

While I pondered our shared human condition, we climbed the outside stairs to the fourth floor flat. I was glad the earlier tension had thawed another degree or two between Dick and I. Marion's thin, sallow face, however, remained shuttered and drawn. She shuffled stiffly behind us, like an old woman in pain.

Her shaking hands managed to unlock and push open the gouged apartment door. But, in the next instant, her silence exploded into fear-powered, hysterical screams. Dick abruptly dropped my bag there in the corridor, and shoved Marion and I up against the hall's cement block wall. After peering around the doorjamb for a very long moment, he cautioned us to stay put, and warily stepped inside.

With one arm around the sobbing woman, I urged her

45

into a few sidesteps. Then I could lean over far enough to peek through the open door myself.

In the Moorish style of the lower economic brackets, the three women had decorated simply, with the sparest use of rustic wooden furniture and a plumply cushioned couch. The only elaborations had been the intricately patterned *Zellig* tiles running around the plain stucco walls at the ceiling line, the carved arabesque screens that used to shutter the one long eastern window, and a once-exquisite example of colorful Moroccan rug weaving on the cement floor.

But the cool simplicity of the room had been violated in every way possible. The pure white walls were smeared with what looked like blood and smelled like excrement. Every piece of wood had been hacked and shattered. Most of the decorative tiles had been smashed.

In the center of the living room, the rug had been slit into shreds, and on top of the blood-soaked rags lay the taut, bloated carcass of a nanny goat. The animal's head and its severed udder, already writhing with insects, had each been stuck up on lamp bases that, in turn, had been set up in revolting display on the breakfast bar separating the small kitchen from the living area. I doubted if anything could live in that room again. It was too full of rage and death.

Marion's sobs had wound into screams again as she leaned in behind me and caught another glimpse of what had been her home. Surprisingly—or maybe not—no neighbor had, so far, come out to investigate.

"Quiet her down! We don't want the police!" hissed Dick loudly from inside the ruined apartment. "I'm going to check out the bedrooms, then we're getting out of here."

Making soothing noises, I backed the shrieking woman into the small ell made by the entrance closet, and gingerly shut the front door, using the tail of my jacket to touch the knob. The smell was a lot stronger in here, but at least the closet partition sheltered us from the sightless stare and gaping mouth of that horrific head.

Marion's unending screams were getting on my nerves,

46

which were not in the best of shape. My stomach was keeping my nerves company by lurching and rolling. If I went ahead and lost my airplane muffin, it wouldn't make the mess in here any worse. But, instead of holding in my own breakfast with it, I clamped my hand firmly over Marion's mouth, and for good measure, pinched her nose closed. A decade of hauling four children and their gear, bucking bales, mucking stalls, and other miscellaneous house and garden chores has left me plenty strong when I need to be.

It worked like a charm for both of us. Concentrating on this project dispelled my own nausea. And, once her air-starved lungs got the message past her mindless fear reaction, Marion automatically struggled to get a breath. Breathing in reverses the screaming process nicely.

As she panted, I stroked her short damp hair muttering assurances, and warning, "Remember, you don't want your neighbors to call in the police."

I understood that if government officials found out about their Bible translation work, or their small attempts at evangelism, it was likely they'd all be thrown out of the country. Permanently. On the other hand, we were obviously going to need expert help to take on some very nasty people.

It was also just as obvious that Marion and I couldn't stay here.

Thankfully, Zubaida had been called away to a gathering at her family home in the north before any of this had happened. Her parents had insisted Zubaida extend her vacation and stay with them out of harm's way.

Dick came round the corner holding a small paisley fabric sack. "I stuffed the things that were still salvageable in here," holding up the pitifully tiny remainder of their belongings. "Come on." He began to usher us out the door, using the fabric in his hand to cover the doorknob. "Let's get out of here. You can both stay with us, or with Alex."

"No!" Marion squealed. I was afraid she'd start in again, but she continued with fearful logic. "They'll do this—or worse—to you or Treva and the girls! I've got to get away . . .

47

somewhere far . . . ." Returning panic rose in her last words.

The man gently put his beefy arm around his trembling friend. "It'll be okay," he promised as he guided her out into the hallway toward the outside stairs. I followed them, closing the door against the revolting scene, and scooped up my own bag.

"I know it doesn't seem like it now, Mari, but God's still in control, and bigger than these devils and their scare tactics," Dick reassured Marion as we reached the cheery yellow bug parked where we'd left it only minutes before. "Remember: 'The Lord is for me, I will not fear; What can man do to me?'" he quoted as he hurried to unlock the passenger door. Despite the tranquil words, his alert eyes swiveled in continuous surveillance.

While he rushed to deposit our bags in the trunk, I climbed in the back seat and Marion dropped heavily into the front.

"What can man do to me?" Marion repeated in a hoarse whisper. "Looks like plenty," she muttered. That was the same verse that had given me courage such a short time ago.

Marion barely turned her head toward me as though a large movement would cause her to fly apart. Her eyes were as vacant and glazed as the goat's upstairs.

"Shay's already dead, you know. She'd have to be—with these monsters. This hasn't been the only warning—just the worst."

Dick slammed the trunk and strode toward the left side door.

"I tried to call you back and tell you not to come," she continued, "but you'd already left. The others have been angry with me for telling you about Shay in the first place. Like it was my fault you'd want to come here and stick your nose in. Like it's my fault these guys are doing this . . . ." The tenuous control was threatening to slip. Tears welled up in her troubled brown eyes.

As Dick checked up and down the street once more, then opened the car door, I put my hand on her shoulder. She shrugged it off and hunched herself down into a tight heap of misery. "I wish you'd never come," she grumbled.

I had reason to wish the same thing.

## 6

Vendors squabbled and bellowed, outdoing the braying donkeys and honking horns. Arms were flung in my face by several salesmen anxious to impress me with their wares. Swarms of small boys buzzed around offering special tours or expensive guidance.

Now, at mid-morning, the crowded market was heating up. Water sellers in their showy skirts and hats, jostled in the narrow streets among the throng of customers haggling over dyed woolens, fresh fruits and vegetables, or hammered metal work.

While school boys sported patterned knit vests with slacks, and younger girls favored sweaters and brightly colored skirts, many older shoppers of both sexes wore a *djellaba*, the all-encompassing hooded robe. Married ladies were veiled; some were entirely concealed behind a white *haik*. A few had even chosen the double veil called a *yashmak*.

I ought to have been that well covered. I could feel hands touching my light-colored hair as I passed. I should have

50

remembered to put my scarf in my purse, but it was tucked away in the tote Dick was clutching as he purposefully pulled us through the undulating obstacle course of the *souk*.

I reminded myself not to make eye contact with people on the street. Women generally won't, but Muslim men, especially younger unmarried ones, are so cut off from plain friendly contact with non-related females that they can be overeager to initiate a relationship with what they perceive to be a more-accessible Western woman.

I wasn't eager for anything except to find out more about what was being done for Shay. If the apartment was a sample of Volcares' handiwork . . . . My heart felt as heavy as the gold and silver camel saddle now being thrust in my unveiled face.

Dick skillfully ushered a pale, silent Marion and me around the next tight corner where we ran straight into the back of a weary, splintered, wagon piled high with slabs of raw, fly-blown meat.

Marion threw her hands over her face with a shriek that was all but swallowed up by the cacophony surrounding us. I put my arm around her again. This time she limply let it stay.

A bent old Arab in a battered *tarboosh*, or red fez, and a skinny boy were wrestling the butchered sides of lamb onto large, black iron hooks. The hanging chunks would soon be on appetizing display in the open window of the tiled booth built into the building beside us.

"*Salaam*, Mohamed," Dick called out, as he inclined his head in greeting.

"*Salaam*, Foster ben Jesus," the toothless shriveled man smiled. He rolled his eyes at the pile of carcasses, then glanced back at the shop. He seemed to be hinting for Dick's help at his task.

"*Inch' Allah*." Mohamed raised his eyes heavenward.

"Not today, Mohamed—" Dick began, shaking his head. Then, he snatched Marion and me back against the booth just in time to avoid being flattened by two large pushcarts propelled through the densely populated alley by running men. Each oversized handcart was heavily loaded with *kesrah*, fragrant, fresh rounds of Moroccan bread. I immediately thought of the baker I'd met once who, because *kesrah* is generally baked in communal ovens, uniquely marked his own products by pressing each unbaked loaf against his belly button.

The sweaty men were shouting, "*Balek! Balek!*" as they rolled full speed through the throng. It means: "Attention!" or "Look out!"

Peeling us off the wall, Dick nodded goodbye to Mohamed, and beckoned us to follow. I grabbed Marion's hand, and scurried to catch up to him. Though I was taller, Dick was quick.

"'Foster ben Jesus'—'Foster, son of Jesus?'" I panted as we jogged along. "He knows you're a Christian?"

Without breaking stride, Dick murmured, "I have worked with him and witnessed to Mohamed and his grandson, Abdullah, there, for three years." Dick's mouth mimicked a rueful grin. "That one reminds me of King Agrippa—'almost persuaded.' But—", the grimace disappeared between clenched teeth, "my chance to persuade him may be over."

Following his swift pace around another corner, I had to pull Marion into the even smaller cobblestone *zankat* lined with high, whitewashed walls which had sheltered unseen residences for centuries. I was grateful to have Dick Foster as our guide.

This *medina*—the oldest part of a Moroccan city—was not only the largest, but also the most confusing of its kind in the country. The Fez medina's winding, mazelike streets have hidden secrets and confounded outsiders since A.D. 808. An unwary newcomer can get thoroughly lost and/or find trouble in short order. I hurried, and urged the shaken, dazed Marion to stay close to Dick, who was really making good time up this unpopulated byway.

So we almost knocked him down when he stopped suddenly

and stood still, staring intently up the narrow *zankat*. Without a word, he indicated that I should bring our insensible companion over to the right hand wall, while he scanned the other direction. Satisfied we weren't being followed, Dick reached out, pushed open a wooden gate in the endless adobe, and urged us inside with haste.

We stepped into another world. Instead of dust and heat, crush and collisions, all accompanied by constant racket, this courtyard garden, or *djenina*, was the epitome of charm and peace. Colorful flowers had been tended through the cooler months, and radiant greenery flowed out from planters built around the thick outside walls. None of the external clatter topped those retaining walls. In here, there was only the soft splash of water in the basin of the stone fountain. Overhanging trees provided a perch for songbirds, who were daintily trilling and chirping their welcome.

This type of shady, watered garden is the average desert-bred Muslim's picture of Paradise. Compared to the sand-blasted, rocky terrain of much of the Maghreb, this *was* heavenly. I could well understand the Arab longing for an eternal oasis.

A green-tiled roof spilled low, forming a small porch that shaded the massive, ornately carved door of the narrow two-story, white-limed house. Before touching the brass bell hanging from a springy coil of wrought iron, Dick lightly took hold of Marion's arm, which caused her to face him. She was still pallid, but the safety of the sheltering garden must have calmed her, too. At least her eyes were tracking again. With a jerky movement, Marion managed to look up into his face.

"Mari. Mrs. Daniels—uh, Eve—" he said, glancing my way. "Until I've had a chance to discuss what's happened with Alex, neither of you," he caught and held Marion's gaze, "is to say anything to anyone in there about the apartment. Can you do that, Mari?"

While she nodded numbly, I started to protest. We needed—Shay needed—help. We had to send out alarms. We . . . .

Dick broke into my thoughts. "The same people that destroyed the apartment have your friend—and ours—Eve. From what we've learned about them over the past few days, what they did there was merely a gentle reminder not to interfere. They're organized and armed. Ready to fight not only with physical weapons, but to control with terrorization. That poor goat could have easily been one of us—including you—if you stay here."

A sob escaped Marion's lips. "I called you Wednesday morning. Early Wednesday afternoon, I found the first letter stuck to our door with a dagger. They put a dead piglet in my car, and . . . and . . . ," her whisper faded. She swallowed hard.

"To put it plainly, the Volcares have threatened to kidnap, rape and mutilate Mari, my wife and girls, as well as Rita, or any other female connected with us in any way. I won't tell you what they've threatened to do to Alex and me.

"They also promised that if we contacted any authorities, they'd send anonymous tips to all the Moroccan ministries concerned with national security until we were investigated and tried as subversives."

"That could mean a death sentence or life in prison," Marion wavered.

Dick patted her arm and shook his head. "Let's not borrow trouble, Mari." He put his discolored ham-hands softly on her trembling shoulders and looked at me. "It would, at the very least, mean we were deported, giving a big black eye to Evancroft's worldwide reputation. Not to mention diplomatic headaches for our own governments."

Marion looked at me, too. "When I got the message that said you were arriving here today, I tried and tried to call you back—to warn you to stay away. But I could never get you again."

No, I had been too busy getting ready to play the heroine. I hate the things, but I began to see a small advantage in using one's answering machine.

"I'm sorry," I said. "I didn't mean to complicate an already

54

impossible situation. But you're not responsible for me or my safety. I came of my own free will.

"And think about it," I heard myself saying, "these guys don't know me by sight as part of your group. Dick, you made sure we weren't followed here today. I know some people, and my way around a lot of the country. I may be able to help more than you imagine." I hoped that was true.

Something like respect was growing in Dick's eyes.

"Maybe it'll be even better this way, than if the whole army and diplomatic corps were involved." I knew my first leading had been the right one.

Dick continued to nod his head. He looked me over as if really seeing me for the first time. Perhaps he was.

"The dilemma, Eve, is that these terrorists say they'll leave us alone if we just roll over and play dead. If we let them have Shay in return for our own safety and the protection of our work here, they say they'll call it even, and the harassment will stop."

"Right! This trustworthy group would never resort to blackmailing you all for the rest of your lives!"

"That, too. But we can't do it anyway. Shay's like another daughter to Alex and me. She's special to all of us. We can't just sacrifice her to these creeps."

"Neither can we lightly sacrifice the work God has called us here to do."

I jumped as the mild male voice spoke behind me. I had been so absorbed in making sense of my strange welcome that I hadn't heard Alex Dawson-Rhys, Ph.D., Th.D.(and a couple of others), open and close the gigantic front door.

Great, Eve. And you're going to use your instincts to hunt down trained terrorist guerrillas.

At least, I assumed that this stoop-shouldered, towering stick of a man now reaching down so delicately to take my hands into his own soft tapered ones, was, as Shay dubbed him, "Dr. D.R.," the scholar, and evidently the owner of this house.

Like the Fosters, the Dawson-Rhys family chose to live

and work within the walls of the ancient medina. However, as Guest Associate Curator of the Museum of Moroccan Arts and crafts, the learned academic worked with his formidable brain, and heart, not his miniscule brawn. His gigantic cue-ball head sat atop bent pipecleaner arms and legs.

But when he smiled his welcome, the kind radiance of it seemed to physically warm my face. The touch of his hands was light and friendly, yet surprisingly invigorating.

"You must be Eve Daniels," he said in his quiet, precise British-English. After introducing himself, he added, "I regret we are meeting under such fearful circumstances. We did not wish for you to unwittingly place yourself in what has turned out to be a very dangerous situation for all of us here. We are not able to offer you much earthly protection."

Something about him convinced me that if heavenly protection was good enough for him, and I could see that it was, it was good enough for me.

"And Marion," he said, turning to her and taking one of her hands while still holding one of mine, "no one blames you for Mrs. Daniels' decision to come. You did what you thought would help."

Marion lifted her eyes and opened her mouth to protest, but the doctor spoke first. "I know there have been harsh words from one or two—" Dick dropped his head and chewed at his lip, "—but those people now regret their hasty temper and wish to apologize later."

Tears welled up in the unhappy woman's eyes and she nodded in relief.

Having set that problem on the road to recovery, the scholar turned back to me. "My dear, if you desire to remain, now that you are fully aware of the jeopardy involved, you are welcome to do so. From what I understand, you are no stranger to this country or its people. You must also perceive that we are in need of all the unofficial aid that we can muster.

"On the other hand, we will certainly understand if you wish to go back to your family and pray for us at home. No one will think less of you for making that rational decision. There is a flight leaving for Paris late this afternoon to which Dick can take you."

Why did he have to mention my family, the kids? I could just imagine Joe's reaction to this hornet's nest in which I'd landed. Of course, he'd be furious over the Volcares' scare tactics. He hates bullies. But then, he also would still, undoubtedly, order me to climb right back on the first plane home.

However, I just couldn't abandon Shay, anymore than these people could.

So, when I told him, Joe'd probably stop hollering directions long enough to listen as I explained that I was scared. And though it seemed impetuous to come here to Shay's rescue, the closer I got to Morocco, the more certain I was that this was where I was supposed to be. There was something here for me to do. Joe wouldn't argue against that. He respects my discernment about God's directions.

Three pairs of eyes were waiting as these thoughts tumbled through my mind. I heard myself say, "God sent me here. I don't exactly know why yet, or what help I'll be to you, but I am supposed to be here. So He'll take care of me as He sees fit. And He'll take care of my family."

Three pairs of lungs expelled held breath. I guess any support is appreciated in desperate situations.

"In that case," Dr. D.R. motioned toward the front door, "please come inside and join our strategy meeting. We've assembled some other friends that wish to assist us. We are going to decide what, with the Lord's help, we can do to get Shay back."

# 7

fra, a dusky servant girl with crossed, downcast eyes the color of chocolate, offered each of us babouches, the pointed slippers always worn inside a Moroccan home. She melted away into the dimness of another doorway carrying our shoes after I had chosen black-embroidered red scuffs embedded with silver-mirrored disks, and tassels at the curved toes. They were a trifle small, but made me feel like a sultana.

"Please come this way," the doctor beckoned.

With his bald pate shining white against the interior gloom, the anthropologist and historian, who, though in his early sixties, seemed to be centuries old. Dr. D.R. shuffled ahead of us down the long cool hallway. Along the walls hung heavy tapestries twining with endless concentric patterns, and a few carpets woven in the bold, bright colors of the *Maghreb*.

At the foot of the steps leading to the upstairs living quarters was a lighted alcove which exhibited a collection of the most beautifully bejewelled and the deadliest-looking curved daggers I'd ever seen. And one sees a lot of these blades, if not all this fancy, about the countryside.

Dr. Alex Dawson-Rhys was an expert in Moroccan handicrafts, both ancient and modern. His knowledge, and, as the scholar himself affirmed, the Lord's intervention, had won him a position on the staff of the museum dedicated to Moroccan works now housed a few winding blocks from here in the *Dar Batha*, the nineteenth century palace of the important Sultan Moulay Hassan.

The doctor's home reflected his love of all types of Maghrebi art, as well as his affection for its people.

But though he had lived here for nearly thirty years, was renowned for his understanding of, and care for all things Moroccan, he was still an outsider. These days, any non-Muslim—any infidel—especially a Westerner, was despised by certain, increasingly violent segments of society. And as an English Christian, the curator qualified on both counts.

Morocco has, in the past, been more tolerant of foreigners, more European in outlook, than many Islamic states. But the rabid, conservative Muslim sects have had their influence here, too, especially in Fez, where scholars from the world over are drawn to study, argue, and make disciples at Qarawiyin University, the Islamic center of learning since A.D. 859. Easily the oldest university in the world, Qarawiyin's *medrassas* (Muslim law and theological colleges), and its mosques have become the birthing place and incubator for zealous groups of fundamentalist Muslims. This school, and other Moroccan universities, also spawn politically active organizations of students with Marxist or socialist axes to grind.

Morocco inherited Ishmael's legacy. Its history is a violent and bloody one. There were short periods of stability accompanied by education, refinement, and the creation of beauty, but they never lasted. Once any sultan or intergenerational dynasty showed weakness, there was rebellion, followed by executions, and new local rulers.

The land of the Moors proved especially difficult for any alien invaders to fully tame. The Romans, Arabs, and French found that geography thwarted their ambitions, because running through the heart of the country from north to south are the three overlapping ranges of the uncompromising Atlas mountains. Only hardy and fiercely independent Berber tribes have managed to live there since before recorded history.

These earliest of all inhabitants of North Africa were called "Barbari" by the Romans because, except for the Greeks, any race other than their own were barbarians to them. Down through the centuries, the word evolved into "Berber." Through it all, the natives called themselves, "Imazighan," meaning: "The Free Men."

No army ever conquered them. They tolerated the Arabs and the French when the benefits gained from a central government didn't much interfere with their own ways. It was by their own free will that they gave allegiance to Allah, and Muhammed, his prophet.

Dr. D.R., our quiet, bespectacled host, wearing a shapeless sweater-vest and frayed white *babouches*, was an expert on the various tribes of these self-reliant and intense people. Therefore, he's also well-versed in the historical wars and native instruments of North African warfare.

Because of Shay, I'd read many of the doctor's papers, often published in American academic journals. In her letters, she had shared, for my edification, several of his goriest recounts of past events. Not too many modern Marocs have cop shows on T.V. with which to entertain themselves. But, they do have storytellers who still hold crowds mesmerized in Moroccan *souks* retelling violent stories of historic heroic struggles. Those are the most exciting. Those are the ones which get passed down.

Shay took great delight in the Lord's plopping her into a culture where a noisy and argumentative temperament is a virtue—at least among males. "It shows His sense of humor, don't you think?" she'd commented wryly.

"Arguing is practically a national sport," she had written during her first year. "The country *souks* are the best. These people would never go to a store and docilely pay a fixed price like well-trained Americans.

"Today Alice took me to the market at Erfoud along the Oued Ziz in the deep south, near the edge of the Saharan dunes," her letter had continued. "With my growing grasp of the main dialects, I overheard a visiting desert tribesman ask directions to some spot up the river. Within two minutes, three different men had gathered and given the poor guy four different answers. For all I know, they are still there arguing over who's right while the nomad headed back to his dunes for some peace and quiet!"

The doctor touched my elbow lightly to break my reverie. "This way, Mrs. Daniels."

I roused myself to start moving again. "Oh, call me Eve, please, Dr. Dawson-Rhys."

"Thank you, Eve. I feel that I know you that well from Shay's talk of you over the years. And I would be honored to have you call me Alex, or D.R., if you prefer."

Finally arriving at the great room, Alex introduced me to the diverse group gathered there, while Dick and Marion seated themselves among their friends with the ease of long acquaintance.

In the center of the far wall where light filtered in through the slit windows, Marguerite Dawson-Rhys reclined on a cushioned daybed. The frail creature was propped up with a plump, embroidered pillow, and swathed in a bright blue woolen shawl, even though the overcrowded room was close and muggy. The lazy whirring of a ceiling fan did nothing to dispel the heat.

She welcomed me with a small, but genuine smile. "Do forgive my not being a proper hostess, my dear. But my strength has not fully returned since my illness." Her slight voice was still melodious, though edged with a dreadful weariness.

I was shocked by her appearance. Shay had described her

61

as a tall, robust woman of great spiritual strength, as well as a scholar in her own right. (I believe she had earned her doctorate in linguistics.) But before me lay a living skeleton.

Last year, Shay had requested prayer as Marguerite underwent a radical mastectomy. Marion worked at the well-equipped hospital in Fez-*Jedid* where she was treated. Believing her place was here, Rita refused to return home to England for the surgery, even though other family was there, including a grown son now teaching at Oxford. However, it was obvious that any medical treatment had come too late for her.

"Eve doesn't mind, Rita. We are all so very glad to have you downstairs with us today," her husband said kindly. As Alex looked at his wife, his eyes were glistening with love and sadness.

I did mind, though, very much. Not her lack of manners, but her dying. With physical health and strength burned away, all that was left was raw spirit. And the gracious warmth of that spirit, the concentrated strength of godliness, the peace of wisdom gained over a lifetime of faith, emanated so strongly from the riveting eyes of the withered figure on the daybed, I could feel them draw me from across the room. The surge of pity within was for myself. That I should never have the opportunity to know and learn from this lovely and wise woman seemed a great loss.

This lady was dying. Shay could also be dying, perhaps was already dead. Yet I have so much life, so much in this life. Marguerite's peace in the midst of this painful, messy existence was a silent and loving rebuke to me.

"You have met Dick. This is his wife, Treva, and their two daughters, Janelle and Lia." Alex went on with the formalities. He was looking to the right of the couch, near Marguerite's head, and was indicating, palm up, a tiny brunette with an ingenuous Shirley Temple smile, and two dark teenage girls who resembled their father. Treva stepped forward out of Dick's encircling arm to shake my hand demurely, while on the other side of their father, the girls, open and curious, bobbed in partial curtsies. Suddenly, I missed Kit and Lyssa. My arms hungered for the warmth of my own daughters.

A dignified old priest in a rusty black cassock glided forward to greet me.

"*Mucho gusto de concerla, mi hija,*" his kind, yellowed eyes crinkled with sincerity. "*Me llamo es Padre Pablo.*"

"*Con mucho gusto, padre.*"

Father Paul was a rarity, a Moroccan Catholic of Spanish descent. He must still be ministering to a portion of the one percent of the country's population that openly professes to be Christian. Of course, a rabbi would be even harder to find here today, although once there was a sizeable number of Jewish residents. I wondered if the padre had dispensation to serve here permanently, or traveled back and forth across the Strait.

Alex forged on as if these introductions were necessary but wasteful preliminaries to the truly important business yet to be done.

Next to the priest, standing jauntily, and uncomfortably close to my right elbow (and sharing the full effect of his fresh, minty breath), was avid Lieutenant Ahmed al-Aziz who, I was informed, was with the Subdirectorate for Internal Security—the intelligence branch of the *Sûreté Nationale*. The cocky officer closed contemptuous tar-black eyes as his smirk bared incredibly white teeth. Clicking his heels sharply, he bent to polish my hand with his bristling mustaches.

Pulling my hand from his wet grasp, I turned my back on him to look farther right, and meet the curt nod of the lieutenant's older fellow *Sûreté* officer, *Capitane* Benanni of the Judiciary Police. The tough captain's pocked face was set in a grim scowl. I sensed he could be a frightening and brutal adversary.

Alex had come full circle by the time he introduced the two younger people rising from divans near Marguerite's feet. The rangy boy in his mid-teens bowed low, and before the doctor could speak, said eagerly, "Most pleased to make your acquaintance, *Madame*. I am your servant, Sami Oufkir. Also to accept my sadness at *Mademoiselle* O'Shea's kidnapping. The *mademoiselle* is my favorite teacher, and the most favorite teacher to my sister, Malika, who most unfortunately—"

"Wait a bit on that, if you would, Sami," Alex's authority cut off the boy's fervid monologue abruptly, though not unkindly. Sami immediately ceased his torrent of English. His tan skin took on a rosy hue as he, with downcast eyes, made another formal bow.

The Caucasian woman in her early twenties, standing on Sami's left, reached out to shake my hand as Alex said, "And this is Robin Moffat. A newly-arrived member of our local Peace Corps team. She has just started teaching English in the secondary school with Shay."

Robin was probably living here. As I understood it, the Dawson-Rhyses' house is always open to visiting missionaries or other foreigners coming to Fez. "Their home is like a harmonious U.N.," Shay had written. "Alex and Marguerite see hospitality as part of their ministry to others."

This houseguest had mousy short curls, a plain, open face with a wide and honest buck-tooth grin. "Glad to meet you, Mrs. Daniels." Hers was an energetic handshake. "Shay has spoken very highly of you. I'm originally from Calgary, you know, Alberta, right up above you in Washington state. Of course, I went to school at the UW in Seattle. That's where I got hooked up with the Peace Corps." She finally stopped pumping my hand.

Living as close to the Canadian border as we do, I recognized the drawn out '*oo*' sounds and the slight clip with which our northern neighbors color our common words. She sounded like home.

"Oh, yes! We visited your city on a trip to that incredible mall in West Edmonton. My children enjoyed seeing the Chinese pandas in your zoo." The need to connect with something familiar and pleasant was irresistible.

"Did you enjoy the three-story Death Drop at the mall's amusement center?" Robin giggled.

"Only my husband would brave that killer—or the roller-coaster. The rest of us spent the day on the waterslides, and surfing the waves at the indoor water park."

"Isn't that a kick?" Robin glowed at the shared memory from home. However, a stray glance at Alex, who was standing behind me, caused her enthusiasm to ebb away. Robin's face closed down with a tight twist of the lips over those protruding teeth. She took a step back and tugged at Sami's sleeve, signaling him to also resume his seat on the divan.

"Marion, you have already met," Alex said, looking at her where she sat circumspectly on the edge of the lounge near Marguerite's feet.

I wondered if she and Zubaida provided the in-home nursing care needed at this stage of the wasting disease.

Marion was holding herself as taut as a guy wire. Her watery brown eyes were still worried by fear. The frenzy had gone, however, and she was resting her hand lightly upon Marguerite's. The unspoken assurances passing thereby seemed to be reciprocal. And Marion appeared to be benefiting from the ill woman's reserves of calm faith.

"Let's get on with this."

I started when Bennani growled behind me in thick, accented English.

"Ah, first we must seat our charming helper," Lt. Aziz purred as he pulled a leather and rattan stool from the front corner and offered it to me with all the panache of an over-paid gigolo.

I crossed to the stool and sank down on it, exhausted. I had no desire to sit so close to the slick and solicitous policeman, but I also badly wanted "to get on with this." Whatever *this* was.

Before I could ask that question aloud, before the gruff captain could get his throat cleared to speak again, the brass bell at the front door jangled.

## 8

Were you expecting anyone else?" Bennani snapped at Alex.

"Well, I . . . . No," the doctor began uncertainly.

The servant girl, her convergent eyesight accentuated by anxiety, appeared at the living room entrance and diffidently spoke to her employer in hasty Arabic.

He answered Efra in a soothing manner. I know very little Arabic, but, I caught something about bringing "tea."

"Excuse me a moment," Alex said to our assembly, and pattered off to answer the door himself. Efra scurried back toward the kitchen clucking her tongue and shaking her head mournfully.

Uneasy silence descended on the room like a smothering blanket. Furtive glances dropped to fidgeting hands. A throat or two was cleared. Across the room, Bennani's scowl deepened as he took out another cigarette. Marguerite sighed quietly and closed her eyes.

Then suddenly, in the arched doorway appeared, the most

wondrous sight my tired eyes had seen in nearly two days.

"Miss Lyndy!"

Ali Bakkali had spotted me, too. He flew across the open space until he stood in front of me, his ebony eyes shining. It was all I could do to keep from gathering him into a big bear hug.

Instead, and more correctly, Ali bowed low with an assured flourish, grabbed my hand, and kissed it quite competently. With an equally magnificent mustache, Ali was much better at hand-kissing than Aziz, who, from somewhere behind me, seemed to be making odd noises deep in his throat.

Ali was much taller, and his shoulders wider than I remembered. But by now, of course, he must be nearing the mature age of thirty.

Time had only deepened those fathomless black eyes that could flash with fire or mischief. Ali had more daring and determination than anyone I'd ever met in my life—including Joe—and that's saying something.

This elegant and prosperous young man standing so straight before me in a sophisticated French suit and Italian shoes wouldn't even be alive, much less thriving, if he hadn't had persistent courage and such an indomitable will.

Ali was a descendent of the Sanhajas, the original proud and adventurous Berber kindred also known as the Veiled Men. They were camelback warriors who conquered the Sahara as well as parts of the Sudan. Their posterity is found scattered throughout the Atlas and the Anti-Atlas, the southern-most range of mountains. Ali's immediate family roamed mainly near the trading town of Goulimine, where Morocco's largest camel market is held annually.

In the early seventies, with a war raging in Spanish Sahara, many of Ali's R'Guibat tribe were no longer able to herd their camels freely about their traditional homeland. Ali's proud, but unprepared father drifted north, eventually bringing eight-year-old Ali and two of his brothers to the capital city of Rabat. He thought there they could find jobs worthy of their abilities.

Instead, they ended up, like so many others, in the *bidonville*. These shantytowns ring most large Moroccan cities. They are slums made of canvas, planks, and corrugated iron scraps that shelter the undereducated country people who migrated to the city looking for work, but who find none, or very little.

The father took to heavy drinking (of course, liquor is officially forbidden by Islam, but where there's misery, there's a way), and gambling, when there was something with which to gamble.

The two older boys made income with odd jobs or stealing. But Ali, severely crippled, made a surprising amount of money by begging—especially from tourists. With his legs and feet knotted and crossed like a pretzel, and a winsome, snaggle-toothed smile on his dirty, handsome young face, he was an appealing beggar.

One day, while working the crowds near *Bab Zaër*, one of the original city gates that lead to the present Royal Palace, Ali solicited money from a touring group of American doctors. Like Peter and John when approached by the temple beggar, the physicians didn't give Ali what he asked for, but brought about a larger miracle that permanently changed his life.

Those doctors, sightseeing on a rare day off from surgeries and clinics, were in Morocco for another children's relief organization, United Missions. Their objective was to provide children around the world with corrective surgeries, not only for life-threatening defects, but also for emotionally painful "cosmetic" deformities.

Ali, knowing his father would never agree to give up his best source of quick cash, saw the chance for his own new life and grabbed it. Once he understood what these men were willing to do for him, ten-year-old Ali, who, like most street kids, knew just enough English, convinced them he was an orphan from a tribe in the northern Rif.

I think the doctors were so excited by the profound benefit

they could offer this eager and intelligent boy, that they risked everything, broke their own rules, and took him at his word.

The disadvantaged are a self-protective lot. They have to be. The disappearance of one beggar wouldn't cause much of a stir, especially one with little family and no tribal ties in the city. Ali knew that when his father or brothers looked for him, they couldn't pursue a search for long. They had no connections and, without him, they'd soon run out of dirhams.

Ali had his first surgery in Fez. One of the group's founders, an orthopedic surgeon named Dr. Allen, took special interest in the boy. He even sponsored him on the next trip back to the United States. Ali was taken into Dr. Allen's own home. Over the next two years he endured the torments involved in scores of surgeries, and therapy sessions.

His quick mind like a sponge, Ali learned to read and write both English and Arabic, and increased his knowledge of French. He also became very attached to the doctor and his wife who, although it was against their own organizational policy, were willing to adopt the boy.

Official adoption proceedings, however, would cause investigations into his family, and Ali was forced to confess he had plenty of family still alive. Since he didn't wish to return to his father, and because he could not be legally adopted and become an American citizen, Dr. Allen worked out a plan for Ali to go back to the Horm School where he could continue to be educated and receive therapy until he became an adult.

On my second visit to Morocco with the Hope, I spent some hours as an aide at the Khemisset school. There I'd met Ali, and promptly lost my heart to the irrepressible thirteen-year-old. It must have been mutual; we've kept in touch ever since, even after he left Horm at eighteen to—

I was jerked back to the present by the bellow of an enraged Bennani.

"By the name of the Prophet! I thought you wished this to be a private affair. How many other street dogs and women have you invited to this tea party, *Docteur*?"

"*Capitane*, everyone here has reason to be discreet. However, this young man said—"

"I invited *M.* Bakkali, *Capitane* Bennai," I spoke up, looking directly into the angry man's eyes. I was tired of him, and tired of not knowing what was going on, and tired of tiptoeing around all the emotional undercurrents flooding this room. I was just plain tired. So I snapped with more bite than I'd normally use in a confrontation with foreign police.

"He's an old and dear friend who knows a lot of people in many different parts of this country. I called him before I left the States and asked him to meet me."

What niggled at my mind as I said this, however, was that I'd asked Ali to meet me at the airport. Why hadn't he? And how had he found me here?

Whatever my private insecurities, my statement told the hotheaded *Capitane* that I was a liberated American woman, like it or not. Hear *me* roar!

Eyeballs rolled. Aziz coughed to cover a snigger. Sami and Robin looked horrified, and I saw Alex frown at Dick, who shrugged elaborately. For several painful heartbeats, Bennani and I played stare down. I had time to pray that I hadn't totally ruined whatever chances were left for Shay's rescue with my own quick temper.

Then Bennani roared back, not in anger, but in thigh-slapping, tear-rolling laughter. He guffawed with his head thrown back in abandon, oblivious to the stunned silence surrounding him. Finally, taking in great gulps of air and wiping away tears with a pristine, towel-sized handkerchief, he gasped, "So, a spitfire! Ah . . . Americans!" He shook his head at Alex. "Perhaps you have done the correct thing after all, my friend."

He turned his rugged, round face to me, now transformed by something like a grin. "I see you take chances, Madame. I hope you are a woman of great courage as well as a quick tongue." His face sobered, but his brown eyes remained soft. "You will need both if you plan to rescue your friend without an army of soldiers and diplomats working for you."

Bennani inclined his grizzled head at me. "May we proceed, Madame?"

I nodded stiffly and sat down.

## 9

This is," the captain continued, "a very large bucket of snakes you have fallen into. I have advised *le Docteur* Dawson-Rhys and *M*. Foster to appeal to their own embassies. Get them to threaten the Volcares with government interventions.

"However, as a friend, I also understand their . . . delicate . . . position here, and their desire to not be exposed to further scrutiny."

Chewing on an unlit cigar, Bennani seated himself on one of the leather divans. Middle Eastern teachers sit down when they lecture; thus he continued to address the group. "We are dealing with a common enemy. Keeping this latest Volcares incident out of the papers would also be beneficial to my countrymen."

Aziz forgot his polish and snorted in disgust over his weak, ineffective countrymen. There must be mounting pressure on the various security forces to put a stop to this increasingly dangerous terrorist group.

As the intelligence officer spoke, Efra finished serving *kab el ghzal*, a sort of croissant stuffed with crushed almonds and rolled in powered sugar; and *atai benaana*, the sweet mint tea of the Maghreb. In a native home, I would be expected to drink at least three glasses of the hot syrup to be polite. I hoped that standard was not expected here. I could barely sip it, much less eat a bite of the elegant pastry.

No one else appeared enthusiastic about the refreshments either. No one except Lt. Aziz, who was downing enough portions for three people. Smacking his lips after his second croissant, he belched loudly.

Bennani persisted with his discourse. "I have agreed, as a long-time friend of *le docteur*, and as a sworn arresting officer of King Hassan in the *Police Judiciare*, with many years experience investigating terrorist activities, to help in this matter—as long as is possible.

"I am ashamed of my compatriots who are afraid to cross these villains for fear of retaliation. However, I have no family to protect. Therefore, I went to my commander and—" Bennani waved his cigar upward—" '*L-hamdo li-llah!*' My superior has given me much authority in this matter. No questions asked. '*Bismillah!*'"

King Cyrus came to mind. He was a pagan ruler who, though an unbeliever, God directed in ways that satisfied His own purposes. "I have also called you by your name;" the Lord said through Isaiah. "I have given you a title of honor though you have not known me."

If the oaths Bennani just made to Allah meant anything, the officer wasn't unaware of supernatural influence, but he was focused now on the material plane.

Bennani went on. "With this authority, I have brought here today *Lieutenant* al-Aziz, whose countersubversion work with our fine intelligence force has given him much knowledge of these Volcares."

Aziz stood and bowed round to his audience.

"Besides, he is the youngest son of my mother's cousin. He will keep your secrets," Bennani said, looking at Alex.

"Your religious beliefs are of no concern to me," the foppish *Sûreté* officer assured us in English ornamented with a suave French trill. "My esteemed uncle has spoken truly on this matter. My only interest in this affair is in capturing and removing these dangerous criminals from our midst." Reading mistrust in many eyes, he tacked on the addendum "— and rescuing your friend, of course."

Bennani yielded the floor to the younger man with an imperial nod. The lieutenant remained on his feet, but constantly shifted his weight from one tightly-sheathed leg to the other with restless agitation. "We believe that the group claiming to have abducted *Mlle.* O'Shea is indeed a unit of the mercenary army calling themselves the Volcares, or," for the benefit of his patently dull pupils, he added, "the 'Overthrowers.' They are based in, and work out of, Spain."

"Unfortunate, misguided souls," Father Paul muttered in Spanish, shaking his steepled fingers against his lips.

"These anarchists," Aziz raised his voice, "have been a thorn in the side of our sovereign state for years now. Recently, however, under new leadership, they have become advocates for specific militant ideologies. They have grown much bolder in their terrorist activities.

"Before, Volcares were known to fight for hire anywhere. Of course, this drew malcontents and criminal riff-raff to their ranks. Now, they are attracting political extremists. They continue to finance their activities with lucrative smuggling operations on various fronts." Aziz ticked them off on his long fingers, "supplying provisions, arms, missiles, drugs . . . whatever a client wants, and can afford to pay."

"No better than an independent Foreign Legion," Dick grumbled.

Bennani grunted his agreement. The squalid reality about the Legion was quite different from the romanticized version Hollywood promoted. Legionnaires are not remembered fondly in this part of the world.

The lieutenant continued. "My surveillance unit has been monitoring the local cell closely due to their apparent link

74

with one of the radical Muslim sects at Qarawiyin. An *alem* there has organized a constant supply line through Spain to the Polisarios."

The black mustache twisted in disdain. "Those stupid camel-herders," Aziz editorialized, "thinking they are great righteous warriors playing Oqba ben Nafi. Since the southern berm was erected, their raids are a lost cause, merely pestering our military forces, squandering money and keeping good men from more important things."

Oqba ben Nafi fought his way across Morocco sometime in the seventh century. At the end of his bloody Islamic quest, he rode his horse straight out into the Atlantic to show Allah (and everyone else) that he'd made good on his promise to conquer the world.

I glanced sympathetically at Ali, who kept a placid face clamped down over the emotions I knew must be exploding inside. The impulsive boy had learned the value of a poker face.

Clan loyalties reign supreme among the Berbers. After his father's death, Ali had, so he'd told me in a letter, restored contact with his large group of siblings and extended family members. Much of his tribe remains in the region of Morocco south of Goulimine. His clan of nomadic herders, the R'Guibats, still call that wide sweep of desert, home.

But the rest of that ancestral home is deep in the war-torn area once known as the Spanish Sahara—now called Western Sahara. Not long after my first stay in the country, in 1975, King Hassan of Morocco organized 350,000 civilians to march into the region. The object of the "Green March" was to pressure a weakened Spain into fully severing colonial ties and to transfer the administration of its Saharan territories to Morocco and Mauritania.

Spain pulled out. But Morocco's monarch found that the Sharawi, the traditional inhabitants of the territory south of the Moroccan border, had already formed the Sharawi Popular Liberation Army. The title in French shortens to "Polisario." They were angrily prepared to fight for independence from any outside government. The Polisarios proclaimed their homeland to be the independent Saharan Arab Democratic Republic.

By 1975, Polisario rebels were supported in their war efforts by Algeria. By 1979, the insurgents had succeeded in winning so many skirmishes, that Mauritania formally withdrew from the war and abandoned any claim to the territory. In the early eighties, rebel forces were receiving sophisticated military equipment, sanctuary, and food from Morocco's other hostile neighbor, Libya. They are still fighting today.

Polisarios are armed with modern four-wheel-drive vehicles, machine guns, and mortars instead of camels and long-barreled *moukkalas*. But, by continuing to employ the *razzia*, the raiding tactics of warfare as practiced by their desert ancestors, the Polisarios were embarrassingly successful in trouncing the first Moroccan troops sent to quell the uprising.

Morocco, with its eye on the pure phosphate ore mined in that part of "the useful Sahara," refused to give up its occupancy. The Moroccan Royal Armed Forces, led by a General Dlimi, countered the resistance by building a "surveillance and obstacle line"—a mined double berm of sand topped with barbed wire, radar, and artillery—that today stretches over five hundred miles from the Algerian border west to the ocean.

Despite incessant attacks from Polisarios using increasingly sophisticated Soviet-made weaponry like tanks and surface-to-air, infrared-guided missiles, the Moroccan army, at the cost of many lives, completed the walls of sand. As long as the interior towns remain heavily guarded, a semblance of peace hangs over the region inside the sand curtain, but the determined Polisario continues to dominate the rocks and desert beyond.

Many southern tribes have members on both sides of this wall—another barrier built in this world by hatred and fear. An estimated ten thousand Moroccan soldiers died before the berm was completed. The years of fruitless attacks on the construction crews also caused the death of many experienced Polisario fighters and sapped survivors' morale. From what I last read of the conflict, probably only about three thousand Polisario raiders remain active in the western Sahara compared to about twelve thousand a decade ago. But it is likely they will persist until they are all dead.

For a Muslim, to die for a holy cause is an honor. Before every battle, the Islamic soldier shouts: "There is no god but Allah, and Muhammed is His Prophet."

Two of Ali's brothers died with the Polisarios in the fierce fighting over a heavily defended town outside the berm in 1981. One of his small cousins had lost his left leg and a hand to a land mine. Several other relatives and friends from the north had been wounded or lost while fighting with the Moroccan Royal Armed Forces.

A fine sweat shone on his unlined forehead and his jaw was clenched down tightly on unspoken words. Wherever his political sympathies lay, I knew Ali hated the berm as a barrier to his inherited nomadic yearning for open space and freedom. Most of his people had never recognized artificial borders or boundaries. Following their flocks and herds, they belonged to the *hammada*, the rocky desert leading down to the sand sea on the western edge of the Sahara.

I always wondered, too, if because of his physically limited childhood, the push to be on the move, to not be walled in, or held back, was even stronger in my old friend.

Heedlessly, the arrogant Aziz droned on with his speech. "We received information late last evening that the Volcares have advertised 'Commodities Up for Bid.' A meeting has been arranged with dealers not only from Libya, but also from the NORAMZA of Mozambique. The exchange is to take place during the Volcares' regular Polisario supply drop at the end of this week."

With friends scattered throughout the world, Joe and I both keep up on current events.

News about NORAMZA was *never* good. Since independence was declared from Portugal in 1975, the "Mozambique

National Resistance Organization" has waged brutal civil war among their own people. NORAMZA tactics include rape, mutilation and torturous murder.

The "freedom fighters" have so disrupted Mozambique's economy there has been mass starvation, especially that of small orphaned children left out in the bush to die alone. Daily, thousands of refugees pour out of the country seeking asylum from the slaughter. The heartless bandits, using mines and rocket-launchers, have killed close to 100,000 innocent civilians and relief workers in the last three years alone.

"This morning, our sources confirmed that the Volcares plan a three-way deal," Aziz was saying. "They made it known they have something Qadhaafi wants, and plan to act as brokers in an exchange of 'goods' between the Libyans and Mozambique guerrillas."

Bennani's rough voice was quiet. "Yes, Mendoza, the new Volcares leader, is branching out beyond the smuggling of Polisario supplies. *Docteur*, we believe he plans to sell your friend, the *mademoiselle*, to Qadhaafi. She will be a hostage he can use as leverage against the American government.

"In exchange, it is likely the Volcares have asked the Libyans to bring a year's supply of poison gas from their new Sabhah plant, so the NORAMZA can continue to destroy their own people in different and creative ways."

"Mendoza gets paid three times for one run, in addition to signing up two new income-producing clients," Aziz added with grudging respect.

I looked up in horror to find Bennani's eyes staring straight into mine. They were still challenging, but also sad somehow.

"Qadhaafi's personal aide, General Oqba al-Qadim, jumped at this opportunity," Bennani went on. "Most likely he has his own personal plans for *Mlle.* O'Shea." Bennani's dark eyes were heavy with warning. "Qadim likes white women."

# 10

Afternoon shadows grew long, but the garden walls held in the warmth of the midday sun. I sat on a tiny stone bench at the front corner of the Dawson-Rhyses' private oasis. The buzzing of bees in the red bougainvillaea overhead, the soft burble from the tile fountain, the long hours of travel and worry added up to a dull heaviness.

I couldn't handle any more of Marion's hysterics, or of the Foster girls' fearful tears, or of Marguerite's deathly white face.

Whatever sympathy there had been moments earlier, it drained out of both officers' faces when they surveyed the mayhem their revelations created. Their smirks said: "This is just what I expected from these women . . . these foreigners . . . these civilians."

In search of some solitary time to think, I'd slipped down the long, dim hall, back out into this garden of light and beauty.

I'm a mother, a housewife, a sometime nurse (when Joe needs help at the office), and a Sunday school teacher. Bennani, though smug about it, had been right. What could *I* do—what could any of us regular non-violent types do to thwart, not one, but three, well-organized, well-armed, and bad-tempered terrorist groups?

I closed my eyes. The light was very bright out here. I meant to pray. But my head was pounding.

*What should I do, Lord? You will have to work a miracle—a big miracle—to get Shay out of this safely . . . .*

And what of my beautiful friend? That General What's-his-name works with vengeful, unpredictable people. What things might he do to her in a kingdom where women can still be used and discarded at a man's whim?

Next thing I knew, someone was yelling my name, and snapping something sharply in my ear. My eyes flew open, and blinked around in the same panic that comes with being caught asleep while the other kids snicker and the teacher, tapping her pencil, stands in front of the class waiting for your answer.

But instead of crabby Miss Mast, Sami Oukfir was peering at me with his face so close to mine, I could feel his rapid breath on my nose.

"*Madame* Daniels, please, I must speak with you," Sami said in a stagy whisper. The surprise and distortion of sleep had made his low urgent voice as loud as a shout.

I was still too befuddled to manage any reply, so Sami took my silence as consent. He plunged directly back into the narrative interrupted during our introduction.

"What has happened to *Mlle.* O'Shea—well, the shame is laid on my family forever. On my father, and on me, as I am . . . *I* was responsible for my sister."

"I . . . don't understand, Sami," I stammered.

"Ah, yes. You as yet do not know. I must go back to the start of this terrible time." The boy screwed up his face in brief contemplation, then began again.

"My sister, Malika, who is only thirteen, and I, who am almost fifteen, attend Moulay Youssef Secondary School in the new city. Very prestigious here in Fez," he added proudly.

"*Mlle*. O'Shea, there is our teacher of the English, and our most favorite. She makes us to laugh in the class, and we go places and learn much from her. Very different from most *fqihs*—the Muslim schoolteachers—you must understand."

I understood. Sami and his sister had fallen prey to Shay's intelligent charm and sense of humor. I suspected adulation was a common occupational hazard for my friend, and Sami, here, had a virulent case of young-love-from-afar.

"Malika, see, she spends much time with the *mademoiselle*. I spend some time helping after school, too, but not so much as my sister. I have more classes, and it is not as right for me as a man—you understand—as for a girl. I do not even mention at home that I still have a lady teacher."

Again, I understood.

"My sister is very interested in why *Mlle*. O'Shea is here in our country. What is her life like back in the United States of America? What does the *mademoiselle* think about many various subjects?

"So *Mlle*. O'Shea, she tells Malika of her belief in the God Jesus—the Christian Three-in-One God—different than Allah of Islam, yes?

"My sister likes our teacher, and she likes her Father God and Jesus. Malika likes the talk of love, of being clean from sins forever, and of knowing you are going to Paradise." Sami frowned. "No bridges to cross just so. No 'maybe's.'

"Beside this," he added, "the power and anger of Allah, and not knowing if she has done enough right things sometimes makes her afraid, Malika says.

"You must understand, my sister is a very weak girl, many times sick. Always, I am told to protect her from the time she was born." Stiffly, he quoted the charge carved into his brain, " '*If she is protected to grow up, she will make very good marriage as we are from important family....*' My father is *ulama* at the Qarawiyin and has much respect." As though someone pulled his plug, Sami's enthusiastic chatter ceased instantly.

Sorting through his words in the unexpected silence, I found two things that surprised me.

If his father was an *ulama*, Sami's evaluation of his parent's social status was certainly correct. *Alems* have attained the highest level of religious scholarship in the Islamic world. They are indeed honored as the most eminent teachers of Muslim law and dogma. To be an *ulama* at a Qarawiyin *medrassa* was to be at the pinnacle of scholarly success.

Obviously, Sami's father was a financial success as well. The boy's expensive European clothing, a daughter attending secondary school, and being able to afford two tuitions for a prestigious private education had already told me Sami was from the wealthy upper class.

That struck me as unusual, for an *ulama* wasn't normally all that rich. They generally enjoyed more prestige than monetary reward.

Most religious officials, like the *imams*, or prayer leaders; the *khatibs* who preach the Friday sermon, the *muezzins* who call the faithful to prayer five times daily; and the *hezzabs* endlessly reciting the Koran, are all government employees. They are highly respected, but their modest salaries would place them in what we call the middle class.

As I studied Sami during his lapse into silence, I also realized how surprised I was by this aristocratic young man's attitudes. Not only did he express true concern about the fate of a female foreigner, but the honest fondness for his sister shone in his expressive eyes. Despite his canned spiel, Malika was far more to Sami than a family asset which, as a male, was his responsibility to protect. He was not the arrogant young man of wealth who, in the Maghreb, is most often detached from beings inferior to himself. Something in Sami still cared with a wistful gentleness.

"So there was much trouble," a subdued Sami picked up his story. "Very big anger when my father finds the infidel book in our house."

"The 'infidel book?'"

"*Mlle.* O'Shea gave to Malika a small part of her holy book. It is a section called, 'John,' written in the French and the English, *comprenez-vous*? . . . so she understand it better.

"Malika brought it to our house to read," Sami was shaking his head miserably at his sibling's stupidity, "and kept it under pillows in the women's rooms where my father would never go. But sometimes she took it in her bag-for-the-books to school to ask questions.

"One day it was no longer in this bag or under the pillows. We looked all around but did not find it. Malika cried for many days after. She was very afraid for it to be found by anyone else—even by our mother or the servants. For they must tell our father.

"Then one . . . ah . . . *l'apres-midi?*"

"Afternoon?" I supplied.

"Yes! One afternoon we were in the garden doing our studies, and I see something under the leaves of a big palm fern. It was the 'John.' This must have come falling out of my sister's bag and gone under the bush. She was so happy and laughing with me we did not realize it was after prayers until my father comes in at the gate.

"My father is a holy man of much great learning. He does not allow for the playing now that we are no longer children. He is very angry and asks to see Malika's book that is making us laugh. I try to say it is mine, but he does not believe me."

Sami looked away, and, for a moment, brushed tapering tan fingertips along his dark cheek.

"My father begins to tear his robes, and scream out against the lies of the Christians that say there are three gods. He shouts against the Great Satan and his devils from the West that are robbing the purity of our children."

Sami's voice faded as he remembered the terrible spectacle. I shuddered myself as I conjured up the image of the outraged patriarch on a rampage. I could practically see the spittle running down his beard, the proud nostrils flaring, and the dilated eyes wild with religious indignation.

"After this, he takes my mother and sister into the house and beats them. Next morning Malika is sent away into the high country to be spoken of no more. Soon, I am to go to the most strict *medrassa*, studying only the Koran and *shari'a* from this time on."

I finally understood what extraordinary turmoil had caused this young Muslim male to disclose such a private family matter to me. His world had been shattered.

He was banished from the school he loved. His beloved sister was now a non-person, if she was still alive. In extremist households, it's not unknown for a woman who disobeys male family members to disappear permanently without too many questions asked.

Then again, Malika could have been hastily given away to a slavish marriage. But, for an intelligent, frail child that would be a living death.

Sami slowly stood up in front of me, holding his chin high and blinking back the threat of tears. Staring over my head, he cleared his throat and began his solemn pronouncement.

"I have left my father and my home forever. Neither will I return to the *medrassa*. I do not understand the Christian God very well. But I like *Mlle*. O'Shea's words of understanding and forgiving better than the hate of my father.

"I have come here to help find the *mademoiselle* . . . to try to make that right . . . and to also try to find my sister. I tell you these dishonorable things because you are *Mlle*. O'Shea's good friend, and I must ask for you to have forgiveness for me."

"Oh, Sami," I said, looking up into that mournful face and wishing I could somehow make his world all right again. "I'm so sorry about your sister and what's happened to both of you. But, what happened to Miss O'Shea is not your fault. You're not to blame."

Sami's eyes fell past mine to look at his feet. "But, *madame*, you yet do not know? It was my father who arranged the kidnapping of *Mademoiselle* by the Volcares."

# 11

The constant hum of the small jets was soothing. But I was no longer sleepy, despite the late, or rather, very early hour. Too much had happened since afternoon. Now the black sky outside served as a backdrop to the cheery array of colored dials lighting the small cockpit.

Among other things, Ali, concentrating on coordinates and radio transmissions, is an experienced pilot. In his position as chief personal aide to the notorious Moulay Ismail ibn Abdallah, better known as 'Barbarossa,' Ali must often transport his wealthy employer to the outposts of his farflung empire. Barbarossa, who's styled himself after the flamboyant pirate brothers that gave the African Barbary Coast its infamous name and reputation, is quite a conspicuous character and folk hero.

"He even dyes his hair and beard blood red like the original owners of the name," Ali had gleefully confided.

I had never met the man—I'm not sure I ever wanted to. But over the years, through Ali's sporadic, but colorful correspondence, I had come to know as many of the tall tales surrounding the modern pirate as did the adoring population of the Maghreb.

My friend delighted in perpetuating, or even enlarging the mythology surrounding his mysterious boss.

"He is a direct descendent of one of the five hundred sons of the terrible despot, Moulay Ismail, the tyrant who tortured or executed any who stood in his way. That left his armies of slaves free to build him the walled Imperial City of Meknés," Ali had written once with verbose relish. "And who am I to dispute his ancestry?" he'd added.

"He took for himself the more refined name of 'ibn Abdallah' when he began the erection of his *dar*—his castle—on the *djebels* overlooking Fez."

That was shrewd, for ibn Abdallah was the founder of the revered Idriss dynasty. His son, Idriss II, built the city of Fez in the early ninth century, and was responsible for its growth as a center of artistic splendor and higher learning.

Where Barbarossa, or his money, actually came from (rumors ranged from gambling establishments in Tangiers to the discovery of buried treasure), I don't think anyone, except maybe Ali, knew for sure. And, if Ali did, he was less than informative on that subject.

However, once Barbarossa's wealth was established, he became a modern-day Robin Hood, balancing a life of ostentatious luxury with great works of philanthropy. Hence his celebrated status with the common man.

And if Barbarossa was the Moroccan equivalent of a mobster with heart-of-gold tendencies, he also seemed to have the proverbial soft spot in that heart for Ali. He had discovered the bright young Bakkali at Horm School, which was built, in large part, because of the pirate's own support and generous contributions. Ali left Horm to become Barbarossa's errand boy the year before Shay arrived at the school.

In my own private scenario, I suspected that the flaming Barbarossa had likewise been a street urchin who, by whatever means he could find, clawed his way out of the gutter to wealth and power. That would explain his treatment of my friend more as a protégé, or even as a son, than as an employee.

A history like that would only increase the affectionate regard of his much less successful countrymen. Though Morocco is less rigid and more European than other Islamic countries, it is still a land of strictly prescribed lifestyles, impermeable class distinctions, and inherited wealth. In the midst of this, Barbarossa embodied the wildly rebellious possibility of change.

The Lear jet whisking us to Marrakesh was the *BarBair II*, Ali's favorite plane from the pirate's private fleet. Back in Fez, Marguerite, Marion, Robin, Treva and the two Foster girls were—Ali assured me—safely ensconced in the high-walled women's quarters with Barbarossa's wives at his impregnable, and well-guarded fortress on the hills outside the city.

In the luxurious passenger compartment behind us slept both Dick and Sami. Glowering and chain-smoking vile, umber cigarettes, Captain Bennani was planted obstinately in his seat as though he dared anyone aboard to try and throw him out.

Worried about Marguerite, Alex had stayed behind to coordinate things with Lt. Aziz. I was much relieved to hear Aziz had more nationwide information available to him at the *Sûreté's* home office in Fez than did Bennani, a captain of the local Judiciary Police.

Whistling a discordant little tune, Ali was still absorbed in his tasks. Needing to get my bearings as much as our pilot, I gazed out the side window at the distant stars.

Since taking Marion's call at home last Monday, I had been drawn up into a fast moving progression of events with serious personal, even international, repercussions. After Sami's revelation, and the policemen's intelligence information, I was no longer ignorant of what had happened to Shay, or of who we were tracking in this rash and desperate rescue attempt.

With Ali's connections and planning we were actually on the kidnapper's trail. No matter how reckless, I had to be part of it. We were Shay's one, slim chance—humanly speaking.

I shifted in my seat, rolling my neck against the tension in my hunched shoulders.

"Are you all right, Miss Lyn—Eve?" Ali asked in his deep voice. A self-conscious smile played around the edges of his angular face. Neither one of us were yet quite used to the grown-up version of the other.

"I'm fine, Ali."

"You could wait for us like the others. I can get good accommodations in Marrakesh. You do not have to go with us into danger."

I assured him that I did. He shrugged his shoulders and went back to his happy whistling.

My mind turned back to the afternoon.


In the garden, Sami had finished explaining that the same night after finding Malika's little gospel, their furious father had stormed back to the university for a strategy meeting with certain fellow *alems* and specifically invited students.

Since the early seventies, when large-scale riots broke out in the major cities, student unrest over government corruption, declining job prospects, and social inequities has encouraged the continuance of reactionary organizations like the radical National Union of Moroccan Students. Many of its leaders have done jail time.

Unemployed *bidonville* youths, and the radical intelligentsia at the universities, swell the ranks of popular Muslim fundamentalist sects.

One such group that combines religion and politics, calls itself the League of Islamic Youth. The League demands an end to corruption, Western influences, social injustice, and the monarchy itself. Officially banned even before their "Jihad Squad" was convicted of conspiracy to overthrow the king, members now continue to meet fervently in secret, in spite of long prison terms or death sentences given to those caught.

It must have been to a queer mixture of men from these, or similar groups, that *ulama* Oukfir took his complaints that night. A rabid fundamentalist himself, but aligned with the *Salafiya* movement, a typically more peaceful group, Sami's father was evidently willing to make whatever moral compromises were necessary to gain retribution against "the emissaries of the Great Satan." The elder Oukfir asked for assistance from men with terrorist resources in order to carry out his angry personal *jihad*.

"Eve. Sami." Alex had padded soundlessly out into the garden at that point in the boy's tale!

"Please, come back inside. I believe you'll want to hear what the policemen have to say."

I must have looked reluctant to leave my haven in the quiet corner.

"The other ladies have excused themselves upstairs. But Captain Bennani would like you to know the rest. Please." The doctor held out his hand to help me up.

As soon as we returned, Bennani and Aziz finished Sami's story.

The *Sûreté Nationale* knew that two of the original Student Union leaders, now out of prison, were working covertly with present student converts, fugitive Islamic Youth members, and outside Communist agitators on a plot to assassinate the king and his family. They planned afterward to step into the breach with their own socialist regime.

Not only were the Volcares from Spain supplying the Moroccan conspirators weapons, training, and leadership; but through the terrorist group, the aging student radicals had also cultivated support for their treason from the expansionist administrations of Algeria and Libya.

When *M.* Oukfir, with all the vengeful righteousness of a Muslim warrior, offered up a vulnerable Christian missionary, and in turn, her co-workers, who all were illegally evangelizing in this closed Muslim state, the foreign *ulama* and Volcare liaison, Adolfo Mendoza, must have immediately seen the inherent commercial opportunities. Mendoza realized that he had laid at his feet a group of Westerners who would not be protected by any organization with political influence, and who could be used to embarrass their governments. Taking any of them hostage would give his group world-wide press and leverage in future demands. Besides, he must have figured doing General al-Quadim a favor couldn't hurt.

Yes, according to Lt. Aziz, Mendoza was one shrewd operator. He was the brains behind the new Volcare squad working out of Fez.

"Mendoza," the lieutenant further informed us, "is a Spaniard ostensibly reared as a Muslim. He has risen to such high position he was invited to teach *Shari'a*, the traditional Islamic law, here at Qarawiyin."

However, although neither Interpol nor Moroccan intelligence had been able to amass enough hard evidence to prove their suspicions, Aziz was more than convinced that Mendoza's primary business in Morocco was as the imported Volcare officer responsible for the now efficient and continuous smuggling pipeline to the Polisarios.

"He has gathered a loyal following of dissidents from the university," the government official said, "and we believe that this 'moonlighting Spanish *ulama*' has honed his disciples into an effective and ominous army. Mendoza has taken this opportunity to branch out into larger markets."

The local cop, Bennani, hadn't resisted a competitive jeer at the national service, even if it was represented by a relative. "Of course, the *Sûreté* surveillance team could not expect the sudden bonus dispatch of *Mlle*. O'Shea."

Aziz ground his perfect white teeth and made manicured fists at his sides. Evidently, his agency had been responsible to watch Mendoza.

The Judiciary Police captain had gone on, "No, the *Sûreté* was anticipating that the arms shipment smuggled into Tangiers last Tuesday would be flown to Algeria on Thursday as

planned. They were caught off guard by the swift and eva-
sive actions taken by Mendoza and his friends."

"How could we realize that this woman's abduction was
related to the terrorists' change of plans?" Aziz had defended
his unit's honor.

"Of course," Aziz added pettishly, "neither was her disappearance reported promptly to *us.*"

What surfaced seemed to be the continuation of an unfinished argument between rival branches of government. Their
domestic squabbling wasn't going to help any of us.

"So, what's happened to Shay? Where have they taken
her?" I asked. Anything to get away from excuses and into
action.

"Oukfir and Mendoza's men followed her from her
evening class—"

"On Mondays she taught a night course for adults," Alex
interjected.

"Yes," Aziz had said, quelling Alex with a hostile stare,
"from the class on Monday night they followed her. Then
forced her car off the road into an alley where they
seized her."

"There were signs of a struggle," Bennani murmured,
studying the gloss on his cumbrous oxfords.

"We believe that they kept *Mademoiselle* in the *medina*
some place as yet unknown to us—until they could arrange
for alternative transport. Then they bundled your friend in
among the Polisario armaments and flew out for Ifrane early
Wednesday morning."

"Wednesday!" I blurted out. Three days ago. "To Ifrane? It's
up in the middle Atlas. I thought they were meeting in Algeria."

"The Volcares realize we are aware of, and are working
together to terminate their activities, *Madame.* Mendoza is
smart. And though insolently sure of his ability to outwit us,
he did not want any risk of losing his most valuable cargo,"
Bennani began, then looked over at his fellow officer. Aziz
took note of his cousin's verbal olive branch.

The lieutenant, somewhat appeased, went on. But he

wouldn't answer my question directly. "*Le fon* . . . uh, *excusez-moi* . . . *le diable* not only moved up the shipment schedule, but he sent out dummy supply teams in various directions, causing us to follow many false leads." It was as close as the pompous officer would come to admitting imperfection.

"At the same time, his university followers began demonstrations in Casablanca and Rabat," Bennani added. "While most of our security manpower was policing riots or chasing false trails, we now know Mendoza began a caravan over the Atlas—"

"—planning to lose any pursuers in winter wilderness." Aziz finished the sentence, not wanting anyone else to deliver the punchline. "He then will steal over the long Saharan border and out into the desert."

"Which way was he headed?" Ali asked Bennani in a nonchalant tone.

Aziz twisted around to confront the new speaker. "The last we have heard it was south, along the western flanks of the Middle Atlas." As if challenged, Aziz had jumped in to respond before the older officer. Suspicious dislike glittered in his black eyes.

It could be a good plan, if they survived. The Middle and High Atlas have peaks rising from 7,000 feet to the 13,661 feet of Djebel Toubkal, North Africa's highest. The rugged mountain ranges still efficiently repel intruders. For weeks at a time, some passes can become impenetrable and supplies must be flown in by helicopter. Tiny Berber villages nearer the summits must cling to life without even that support.

Once over the top, as you travel eastward, the inhospitable mountains peter out into that vast and hostile sea of sand—the Sahara. The harsh vagaries of nature in both mountain and desert are quick and deadly.

Something bothered me. "What do you mean, 'He *will* steal out into the desert?' Don't you mean he'll *try*?"

"There has been no formal complaint of kidnapping, *Madame*. Evidently, you intend to make none," Aziz's lip curled in contempt. "Our superiors have called off the pursuit as a waste of time. All agents have been reassigned to identifying and arresting student dissidents. My unit has been ordered to wait and intercept the Volcares' next smuggling run."

"If we wish to rescue the *mademoiselle* before Mendoza reaches his unknown desert rendezvous, we are on our own." Bennani muttered.

Having foreseen this development, Ali had already slipped away.

12

On the heels of Bennani's dismal pronouncement last night, Efra had popped into the room and anticlimactically announced dinner.

Before the poor girl could finish serving the despondent household the evening meal—*harira* (a thick soup of tomatoes, peppers and olives), oranges, freshly baked *kesrah*, and *couscous* (boiled grain that looks like rice and flavored with spices till it tastes like noodles)—Ali returned.

During his absence, he'd made arrangements for every woman here to have safe lodging in Barbarossa's *dar*; set up meetings with an informant, a guide, and an outfitter in Marrakesh for early *this* morning, and had the Barbair II gassed up.

I delight in the foods of different cultures—with certain exceptions. However, Moroccan cuisine has always been one of my favorites. At that dinner, I'd had to choke down the few bites I could manage. Added to already tense circumstances, the argument at the dining table hadn't been conducive to good digestion.

At least the policemen left before it started. Seeing others more powerless than himself had restored Aziz's good humor. With a bow and a flourish, he departed, leaving behind the tentative, but welcome release you get when an aspirin finally takes effect on a nagging headache.

Bennani followed Aziz, but only after one last, hushed conversation with Ali, Dick and Alex out in the hall.

When the three men returned to the table, Alex announced, "We must continue to wait for a miracle.

"We have friends around the world praying for Shay's safe return. And we have not yet exhausted all possibilities from friendly diplomatic powers."

A pacifist, Father Pablo agreed with him.

Dick and Sami both loudly advocated personal action.

"I climb and ski those mountains. And I've done dialect work with both the Ait Seghrouchere and the Beni Mguild tribes. I can get around pretty well up there," Dick began.

"And it is my duty to avenge the Oukfir honor," Sami added.

"We might be able to catch up with the kidnappers in the mountains, or the *hammada*, before they reach their reinforcements in Algeria." Dick continued.

"And do what? Walk into the Volcares camp and politely request that they turn Shay loose?" Treva spoke up with surprising vehemence

Marguerite had remained upstairs so she didn't have to face this additional stress. Marion and Robin had taken trays back up and stayed with her.

"Or are you going to go in with guns blazing and ambush trained terrorists?" Treva's voice trembled with anxiety.

Dick's daughters' eyes widened in fear. Sami, on the other hand, was so thrilled by that idea, that his whole body joined his head in nodding up and down.

"Treva!" her husband cried.

"You know what you said after Vietnam. Especially now with your Christian witness here."

Dick scowled. Tearfully, Treva subsided.

Ali rolled his eyes back up into his head. That must have been why he kept shaking his head over and over —to knock them loose again.

But Dick wasn't finished with Treva or Alex. "I *have* prayed and I think the Lord wants me to go after her. Actually, after what Bennani just told us, I *know* I have to."

Behind his bifocals, Alex's faded blue eyes darted toward Dick with disapproval. Or was it warning?

Dick wasn't used to making speeches, but his conviction wouldn't allow him to keep silent. "Maybe we can't call out armies and all, but God doesn't necessarily want us to sit on our hands, either. What about the shepherd with one lost sheep? Didn't he search for the lost one until he found it?

"God's perspective isn't like ours. Every child of His was— and is—worth dying for. Sometimes, He asks *us* to risk everything."

Dick turned to his wife, "Treva, we said before we came here, that we were willing to give our lives to do this work. Now the Lord is holding me to that promise, and to trust Him for the outcome . . . not a gun."

"You're right, Dick . . . I'm sorry. I'm just so frightened—" Treva opened her hands up and out in silent appeal.

"I know, sweetheart," Dick said, as he collected both of his wife's shaking hands in one mammoth palm.

At that point, Ali pulled me aside. "*Madame* Lyndy—"

"Ali, we're both grown-up now. Call me Eve, please."

"Okay. Yes, *Madame* . . . Eve. While your friends here debate and pray, your other good friend is being taken ever farther from us. Since you asked my aid, I took it upon myself to have made arrangements for a small group of . . . how do you say? . . . 'guards of Barbarossa' . . . to meet with me.

"Also, there will be a guide and an . . . ah, information seller . . . in *Djemma-el-Fna* in the morning at five o'clock." He had glanced at his gold Rolex. "This is seven hours from now.

He held a long finger to his lips as I opened my mouth,

and continued, "I want you to understand these are not nice people I am going to track through the mountains. The companions I have asked to accompany me are not . . . nor am I . . . afraid to use, ah, force, if it will get your friend back."

I'd been waiting for this all along—the call to action. That's probably why it occurred to me to ask Ali's help in the first place.

"I'm coming with you."

Mother had often accused me of being impulsive. I still felt the sting that word left as she'd flung it at me like a slap over the years. She had hurled that adjective, and a good many others in disapproval: foolish, stupid, heedless, impractical . . . .

"Only an American woman would say this!" Ali crowed. "You think you are that lady cowboy from the Wild West?"

"Who? Calamity Jane?"

"No matter. I knew that you might want this. I have seen you fairly brave."

During my time at Horm School, I had run into a few hostile Muslim fathers who failed to appreciate the therapy offered their children. I'd also had to stare down one or two of the older, streetwise pupils.

"Can you shoot?"

Living out in the country as we do, where I'm often alone with the children, Joe had taught me to shoot his old .22 caliber rifle.

"So at least you can fire warning shots in the air and alert the neighbors or scare bad guys or rabid dogs away without killing yourself or one of the kids," were his exact words.

Joe wasn't being chauvinistic, just realistic. Guns had always terrified me. And I wasn't too swift with knives in the kitchen. Or rather, I was too swift for some of my fingers, which he'd had to stitch up. He had good reason to worry.

But I'd fooled us both, and turned out to be—well, a competent shot, anyway. Must have come from my mother's talent with skeet. Or her deadly aim in verbal volleys.

However, though I'd mastered the use of the weapon, I kept it buried under lock and key in my private attic cache, and prayed I'd never have cause to dig it out.

"Yeah, I can shoot," I finally responded to Ali's question. "But I don't think I could ever fire a gun at a human being."

"*Inch' Allah*," he said piously, despite the malicious smile creeping over his handsome face, "you know we say 'as God wills.'

"Yes. Of all women I will allow you to come. But you must not complain. And we must certainly cover your hair."

Under Ali's appraisal, I felt like a squatty burro with mange auditioning for a comic part in the wild *fantasia* charge of magnificent Arabian war stallions. But backhanded as his acceptance was, it was a vast compliment. I tried to take it as such.


My ears were popping. The plane's flaps let down with a jolt. Sitting up with a yawn, I saw the stars beyond Ali's head disappearing as the inky blackness began to dissolve into the dove-gray wash of morning.

Stretching out cramped legs and numb fingers, I took stock of my situation: Here I am, Eve Daniels, in the cockpit of a Moroccan gangster's private jet, descending through the Sunday dawn, toward a mysterious rendezvous in Marrakesh's renowned *Djemma-el-Fna* square.

Though now it's a vast and lively marketplace, *Djemma-el-Fna* means 'The Assembly of the Dead.' I hoped it wasn't a prophecy.

# 13

*Djemma-el-Fna* isn't truly square. It's more a huge, triangular gap inside an enormous medina.

Its macabre name comes from the time long ago when this open space was used to display each week's collection of heads the local governor had gathered from felons. The idea was to discourage others with criminal tendencies.

Despite its dreadful name, which—if you don't know what it means—sounds quite delightful rolling off an Arabic tongue, the place is home to one of the most animated and entertaining bazaars in Morocco. All day long the ever-changing, clamorous parade of peddlers, shoppers, porters, scribes, nomads, beggars, storytellers, musicians, dancers, snake charmers, water-sellers, acrobats, sword-swallowers, fire-eaters, monkey handlers, and foreign tourists flow by like the world's biggest circus parade.

Now with the sun rising in earnest—the pink glowing from rooftops and lighting each of the surrounding minarets one-by-one like giant birthday candles—*Djemma-el-Fna*, quiet through the night, was coming back to life.

In the winter morning chill, I sat at a miniature table outside a little cafe, sipping steaming *café au lait* from a chipped china cup. Shopkeepers across the way were pushing back bulky wooden shutters, opening for the business of another market day.

Friday is the Muslim day of worship, not Sunday. So the market of the day would be . . . *Souk el Had* . . . the Sunday, or first market.

Itinerant merchants were scurrying about, setting up moveable stalls. Soon they would offer their cheap jewelry or flimsy, shiny souvenirs. Later on almost anything imaginable could be purchased somewhere in this *souk*. From old candy bars to transistor radios, from fine leather luggage to items of silver and gold, from hashish (or *kif*) pipes to daggers, from perfumes to tacky plastic gimcracks, your heart's desires could be bargained for here.

The early brisk breeze carried mingled scents from hundreds of small charcoal braziers. I caught whiffs of simmering seasoned soups full of mutton, chick-peas, and eggs; hot lemon chicken with olives, sizzling fried fish; and the spicy little lamb sausages eaten off long skewers.

Tantalizing yeasty odors wafted out of the bakery next door. Besides bread, there would be honey cakes, *baklava*, and probably thin pastry sheets destined to be part of the one hundred and four layers in someone's specially-ordered *bstila*. *Bstila* is a party masterpiece stuffed with pounds of butter, thirty eggs, chopped pigeon meat, sugar, almonds, and seasoned with cinnamon, ginger, saffron, and onion.

However, when the wind changed, the camel and assorted livestock odors—from the nearest *caravanserai* where traveling tribesmen parked their bellowing, grumpy steeds beside an amazing array of trucks, buses, and wagons—overpowered the infinitely more appetizing smells of food.

My cold, offended nose dove again for refuge into the warm, sweet aroma of my creamy coffee.

Before full daylight hit the hard-packed dirt street, a nasal wail knifed through the muted morning stirrings. I was startled by the first call to prayer from the *muezzin* in the Koutouba minaret. His dissonant chant scratched out through a loud-speaker on the splendid, forbidden tower that rises two hundred feet over Marrakesh. From up there, the view of the city's lovely gardens, and the snow-capped mountains beyond, must be quite a sight. But only the chosen few will ever see it.

Some of the faithful around me whipped out their folding prayer mats where they stood, and, heads toward the East, got down on all fours, putting their faces to the ground. Others left their tasks and walked toward corporate services at the neighborhood mosque.

One elderly water carrier was having great difficulty displaying devotion to his god.

Those peddlers have always had my sympathy, even if they still only dress so extravagantly to make money from tourists eager to snap their picture.

As they wander through the crowded *souks* selling drinks of water to thirsty shoppers (and posing for pictures), they wear colorful, but uncomfortably hot costumes with full skirts and leggings. Besides hauling large goat skins heavy with water, and rows of hammered brass cups attached to leather shoulder sashes; these men also balance high steepled hats with gigantic flat brims that dangle two rows of long red tassels in their eyes. Their faces are often covered with white wrappings and their leather vests are smothered with sewn-on coins. Completing the look are woven sashes, and red and green embroidered pantaloons. Some sport curved elfin slippers. Just putting on that outfit each morning would ruin my disposition.

It took the sincere old man so long to divest himself of his burdens that prayer time was half over before he managed to creak down onto his portable mat. But once there, he bobbed up and down in a quivering double-time to catch up. I tried not to watch him.

Sometime before the *muezzin's* call, while I was being entertained by the sights and smells of the Square, Ali, Dick, and Sami had disappeared into the shadowy interior of the minute cafe hoping to retrieve some solid food for breakfast. Now that we were on the move, my stomach had unknotted and was loudly grumbling about my lack of attention yesterday. But, starving or not, everything would wait until prayers were completed.

Aware of the old Muslim honoring his beliefs in the dusty street, I thought of the pocket-sized Bible tucked in my flight bag. My own daily devotions suddenly seemed urgent and appropriate.

As the Arabic words of the Koran floated over my head, the first words of Psalm 27 sprang into my mind:

> The Lord is my light and my salvation;
> Whom shall I fear?
> The Lord is the defense of my life;
> Whom shall I dread?

A resigned Alex had spoken those verses as his blessing when he saw us off in the dark hours of this new day.

I flipped to the middle of my slim, burgundy-colored Book, found the place, and continued to read:

> When evildoers came upon me to devour my flesh,
> My adversaries and my enemies, they stumbled and fell.
> Though a host encamp against me,
> My heart will not fear;
> Though war rise against me
> In spite of this I shall be confident.

Verse eleven jumped off the page at me:

> Teach me Thy way, O Lord,
> And lead me in a level path,
> Because of my foes.
> Do not deliver me over to the desire of my adversaries;

> For false witnesses have risen against me,
> And such as breathe out violence.

Good old David. A man after God's own heart. God Himself called David that. Yet the Lord's anointed had fought and even killed people in battle. David had known what it was like being threatened by violent men. He'd asked, and been given, God's help to defeat them. Of course, as a man of violence he had also been denied the privilege of building the Temple in Jerusalem.

Then came my favorite part of the Psalm—the promise:

> I would have despaired unless I had believed
> that I would see the goodness of the Lord
> in the land of the living.

On *this* side of heaven, I thought. Even in the Square of the Dead.

> Wait for the Lord;
> Be strong and let your heart take courage;
> Yes, wait for the Lord.

*I am waiting on you, Father. I asked for Your guidance from the beginning of this nightmare, and I believe You've brought me here, ready to take off to search for Shay. If I'm wrong, shut the door. Show me what to do. Please protect her and keep her safe. Help us to get her back without any bloodshed. Teach us Your way. Show each of us what to do next . . . Where to go . . . .*

"Eve . . . would you like a croissant? Eve? Afraid it's yesterday's. Too early for fresh. Are you all right?" Dick's questions broke into my other conversation.

I opened my eyes. He and Sami were back with hands full of semi-stale rolls and a fresh pot of the milky coffee. The old water carrier, all put back together, was jangling as he hobbled off in search of his first customers.

Back in the dim restaurant, Ali remained in earnest conversation with a Saharan Touareg who had leathery brown skin and a hooded expression. Next to that sly, white-robed figure was planted the massive, silent black form of a Harrantine. Swathed in ebony robes, only the whites of his half-closed eyes were visible through the interior gloom.

Dick caught sight of my Bible and realized what I'd been doing. I cut his apologies short, though. My spirit was refreshed, but my flesh was weak.

As we three worked our way through the pile of day-old pastry, I realized my spiritual hunger had also been satisfied. I recognized the reassuring peace within. A terrifying unknown lay before us, but my heart was full of courage and conviction.

I needed that inner peace over the next few hours of hectic activity, since both my convictions and my courage were about to meet their first tests.

Whatever information Ali's sinister-looking informants gave him only fanned the flame behind his shining black eyes. He was enjoying himself immensely.

"What did the Touareg say, Ali?" I asked when he pulled over a wrought iron chair, straddled it backward, and joined us at the table. I pushed the plate with the two remaining croissants toward him.

Sami devoured the rolls the instant Ali waved them away. My friend's energy was not coming from bread. Challenge and danger were feeding his inner fires now.

"*Madame* Lyn—Eve, do you trust in me?" Hands outstretched, Ali answered my question with two of his own.

"I know you ask your god what to do. It is true, I have not always been the most holy person. If he is a god, he must know this. And you must also have guessed. What does your god tell you to do about me?" he concluded with an angelic look on his unlined, forthright face.

"Why, Ali?"

He jumped off his seat like he was propelled by an

overwound spring. Then he bent down over me until he was so close, I had to pull back my chin to bring him into focus.

"Will you put your life—the *mademoiselle's* life—totally into my hands in the coming days? Can you and your friends, here," his sweeping gesture took in the man and boy, "follow me where, and when I say?"

Dick and Sami looked at each other, then at me, waiting to hear my response. After all, *I* was the one who claimed to know this man who was planning to lead us into a rugged winter wilderness to face armed criminals.

I studied *Ali's* apparently sincere and handsome features.

I had known the boy. The boy who had grown up among thieves and beggars and liars. The boy who had learned to take selfish advantage of every situation in order to survive.

How well did I know this man before me who worked hand-in-hand with a shady, probably felonious, character?

Did Ali really know what to do in a situation like this?

Did we have any other choice?

"I trust you, Ali," I said quietly. "I can't speak for the others. That's their choice. But God has promised to guide me. I've trusted Him to do it, and I believe He's brought you to us.

"Who knows? Maybe I met you all those years ago so you could help me, and Shay, now."

I surprised myself with such a courageous speech. It would have been perfect in a Spielberg adventure movie. But this was the real world, and the men we were preparing to follow shot real bullets.

Dick had made up his mind as well. Both he and Sami leapt to their feet. "Where do we start?" Dick said. He seemed glad to be on the move.

I stood up too. "If we're heading into the mountains, I'll need to call Joe."

"We leave in two hours. You must all be properly prepared first. Then you may call your *pasha*. . . . After you, *Madame*."

Ali winked as he bowed and gestured the way toward the shops he had in mind. His slight limp didn't slow him down at all.

## 14

Joe was one cranky *pasha*.

It always did take him a few minutes to warm up to new ideas. Or longer. And, of course, I had to take into account the fact that he'd, just moments ago, been sound asleep.

"You're *what*?"

Over the fizzing long distance connection his voice boomed. I pulled the ancient telephone receiver farther away from my eardrum.

"Have you lost your mind? I didn't send you off to Morocco to get killed—or worse! You were only going to lend moral support . . . comfort . . . you know . . . . Who's going to comfort me—and *your* children—when we get your body back in a box? *If* we get a body back!"

I shivered in spite of the closeness of the little shop. The small brazier here at the back not only heated the narrow stall past comfort, it also filled the air with an acrid haze that made my eyes water.

The shopkeeper, who had agreed with Ali to let me use his 1950's vintage pay phone for my overseas call, kept a suspicious watch on me. I turned my back on his curious stare, and tuned back in to Joe's tirade.

" . . . dare chase off after those maniacs with a group of strange men led by this guy you only knew as a kind of a juvenile delinquent and who now works for the Moroccan mob! What if he plans to sell *you* to Shay's kidnappers?"

My new brown wool *serwhals*—pants the mountain villagers often wear, which hang loosely around the hips, but taper in tightly from calves to ankles—were stiff and prickly, and my newly purchased cropped black wool jacket was making me uncomfortable in this heat. I shifted my weight and scraped at my left leg with my right fur-lined leather boot.

In the end, I never got a chance to answer Joe—even if I could have. Before I could get a word in around my husband's angry shouts, the impatient merchant, with one alert eye on potential customers sniffing around the copper wares and iron work jammed in every cranny from floor to cciling and spilling out into the dusty street, took matters, and the telephone, into his own hands.

The greasy little man, in his limp, striped *djellaba*, must have misunderstood my twitchy, teary-eyed silence, and the manly bellows erupting from the receiver. Ali evidently hadn't paid the trader enough *dirhams* to cover excessive long-distance charges run up during an intercontinental argument while he took the time to bargain a sale. (Lengthy transactions often require a merchant to leave shop premises in order to run after, and woo balky customers back with a smile, and the stock promise: "For *you* special deal!")

Cackling at me in gritty Arabic, the owner snatched the receiver in his grimy brown claw, screeched a curt farewell at my exasperated husband, and slammed the handpiece back down in its cradle. He wedged his short stringy body between me and the big black wall phone. Then, with thin arms outstretched, he began to herd me out of his booth with a bloodshot scowl and toothless hisses.

Out in the blinding glare of mid-morning sun, I blinked back over my shoulder to see him descend upon two stout English ladies in sensible shoes. Leaving the shopkeeper to his fate, I turned in time to dodge a flock of porters carrying poles hung with long, gaudy loops of dyed wool for the *medina's* rug weavers.

Dick, outfitted in his new native mountain gear and pacing a tight circle of impatience, was waiting at the barber's corner as planned. Sami, dressed also in *serwhals* and turban, stood transfixed at the hub of Dick's circuit. He was entranced by a ritual as far removed from his urban world as it was from mine.

All the barbers were extremely busy this morning out here in the open, shaving the heads of a cadre of newly arrived tribesmen. Bald, except for a single lock of hair, these desert dwellers believe that when a Muslim soldier dies fighting for his faith, Allah will grab that hank of hair and pull him into paradise.

For a Muslim, attaining heavenly bliss is never a sure thing. You don't know, until after death, if Allah, with capricious grace, will allow you to be one of the lucky ones to safely cross the final bridge over hell. So these warriors hang onto their hair-pulling promise as the closest thing to assurance a follower of Islam ever gets.

"Well, how did it go?" Dick asked perfunctorily as he started to stride off toward the *caravanserai*. He tugged at Sami's woolen sleeve and the boy followed after a few more backward glances.

"As well as can be expected," I mumbled miserably. I was still determined to go, but Joe's reaction had depressed me.

Jogging along with Dick's anxious cadence, I tried not to think about dying.

I knew my God didn't need it, but maybe it was a good thing *my* hair was pulled into a short ponytail under the black linen veil Ali had insisted I wear. Easier to grab.

"Kef Rala has heard much in the mountains about Mendoza and his men," Ali was explaining.

Our well-loaded caravan of land rovers, trucks, and horse trailers was making good time as we headed back north into the hills to Khenifra. It seemed like we'd been on the road for days, but it was still Sunday, only seven minutes after noon.

Once again I was flying beside Ali—although this time we were mostly earthbound in the lead four-by-four. He was averaging at least eighty on highway P24 where it skirts the foothills of the High Atlas range. Since the roads were reliably plowed along the Khenifra cutoff, we would probably reach the pleasant, tree-lined headquarters of the Zaiian tribe on the banks of the *Oum-er-Rbia* close to one o'clock.

The sun had been left behind in Marrakesh. Here, thick gray clouds lowering overhead were spattering the windshield with light rain. They would be spitting snow in the higher elevations.

"After arriving with their shipment in Ifrane last Monday night—Kef Rala was told—the Volcares were seen making camp in the forest of Ain Leuh," Ali continued with his third-hand report.

The village of Ain Leuh lies at the center of a dense forest of pines, green oaks, and lofty, centuries-old cedars. Just south of the village stretches a lonely wilderness inhabited largely by stream trout, and a prolific gang of crabby monkeys who'll accurately hurl any handy object at humans invading their territory. The Volcares would fit right in.

"Kef Rala," Ali went on about the Touareg I'd glimpsed in the Marrakesh cafe, "tells me he hears Mendoza was in Khenifra last Friday, buying many Zaiian horses, at large prices, for a mountain trip."

I hoped Ali would finish his disjointed account before we arrived at our mountain destination. If we ever arrived.

Ali used his hands to gesture constantly as he talked. Joe and I like to drive fast, too. But at least Joe watches the road.

" . . . very unusual during such a cold winter," Ali was saying like a man puzzling out loud to himself. "Even though the high price was also meant to buy silence from the horse traders, word of such a curious happening was bound to get out.

"Had to be the women," he concluded, after a moment. "They bear quick tongues *and* long, dull winters."

I threw him a dirty look. But for once he was concentrating on the slick, curving road and seemed unaware of my reaction.

The Zaiians are vigorous horsemen who breed fast, sturdy stock for their beloved wild races. If any horses were up to winter mountain treks, Zaiian steeds would be. Thinking about it, I would guess that the beautiful horses loaded into our own trailers hitched behind each land rover had blood from this tribe's champions.

" . . . even more dull than usual this year since it has been so very much colder," Ali picked up the thread of his last thought.

Way back in Fez, in what seemed like the distant past, Alex had mentioned worriedly that this had been one of the worst winters in many years, both in terms of low temperatures and record snowfall.

I'd always had to fight incredulity that when I was in these rugged mountains, I was actually on the African continent. On the other side of these peaks now looming over us— peaks that boasted major ski resorts—was the edge of the Sahara, the hottest place on earth.

"My cousin in Khenifra told me that last night it was again minus twenty-two degrees. Of course, it will be even colder higher up."

I was horrified until I remembered Morocco is metric. I calculated roughly that if thirty-two degrees Fahrenheit is freezing, and that's zero on the Celsius scale, minus twenty-two was close to what we'd call five below zero. Bad enough, but not as bad as it first seemed. It cheered me, even though on both sides of the highway, the frozen heaps

110

of plowed snow piled higher as we climbed upward.

"You have a cousin in Khenifra?" I asked. I wouldn't think about the cold. Or if Shay was warm.

"I have 'cousins' in many places. I come from a very large family." Ali winked at me and beamed his broad smile.

"And this 'cousin,' hearing I am interested in further news about the horse buyers, sent out one of his own sons to follow tracks back to Mendoza's camp. Tewfik, the son, is good in the trees like one of their monkeys. He stays long enough to hear them plan their route . . . ah, how do you say?"

Ali released the steering wheel completely so he could clasp his hands together and wriggle them back and forth.

"Zig-zag?" I gasped, as the land rover veered directly for the mountain's edge.

"Ah, yes, zig-zag over the mountains toward Imilchil."

Ali grasped the wheel again in time to not only avert a plunge down the hillside, but also to swerve back into our lane, avoiding a head-on collision with the white Mini hurtling south around the same hairpin turn.

"This zig-zag trip to Imilchil is meant to discover if they are being tracked. Which—Allah be praised—they do not believe, because of the student riots they set off, and their false trails, and the *mademoiselle's* . . . ah . . . delicate predicament with the governments.

"Abu Talib says Mendoza is headed toward Taouz oasis where, both he and your policeman, Bennani, have heard, Algerian fighter jets have been alerted to make a quick run across the border late this week."

"Wouldn't it be better to be waiting for them there than to try to catch them in the mountains?" I asked, half-embarrassed. I felt like a kid playing cops and robbers.

Ali knew this was no game. "No, *Madame*," he said seriously. "We cannot be sure that is their destination with your friend. And there would be no way for us to conceal ourselves from them, for the desert has many eyes.

"Abu Talib agrees that our only chance is to surprise them in the mountains."

"Just who are Kef Rala and Abu Talib, Ali?"

I thought uneasily of the stealthy nomads who were riding in one of the other trucks with Dick, Sami, and Ali's men.

Our scowling, smoke-wreathed friend, Officer Bennani, however, was not back there. He had mysteriously disappeared before breakfast in Marrakesh and never returned. I didn't know whether to be relieved or concerned. I'd have to remember to ask what happened to him.

But there were too many other vital, unanswered questions.

"How do you know you can believe what they tell you?" I said, completing my last spoken thought. "They must keep some rough company to have 'heard' all these plans made by terrorists."

Ali's private, pirate grin returned. "So . . . so . . . . If that is true, they also better understand what the holy Koran teaches: 'Whoso commits aggression against you, do you commit aggression against him.'

"Much better in my world than your womanish Bible, eh?"

When I didn't take the bait, he went on, "Besides, they also understand my money as well as power."

## 15

*Clack . . . Clack . . . Clack.*

"*Madame* Daniels." . . . *Clack* . . . "Please to be rising." . . . *Clack-clack* . . . "We must be off again in twenty minutes, says *Monsieur* Bakkali. Thank you very much."

"Okay, Sami. Be right there," I said, trying to shake some feeling back into the arm I'd slept on. It was still asleep.

The boy, on the other side of the large boulder, was tapping rocks together so I wouldn't miss his summons over here in my segregated little cove.

Part of me wanted closer human proximity last night when we made camp in the forest. But societal restrictions must be maintained. After considering most of my present company, I decided I welcomed the limited access.

Dick had helped me build my own small fire, and had promised to sleep on the other side of the boulder, "to guard the harem entrance," as he put it.

Sami, caught up in the throes of hero worship, had deserted

me to tag after Ali like an exuberant puppy.

Ali had given me a Smith and Wesson.

The overcast sky displayed the soft silver that precedes full sunrise. On tiptoe, I reached up toward those clouds, then bent over and tried to massage out some of the ground-in kinks. It hadn't snowed in the night, but I began to shiver as the warmth from my sleeping bag dissipated in the gusts of icy air.

I wondered briefly how Shay spent the night, and I took a moment to speak to the Lord.

Ali, Dick, Sami, the two mysterious Arabs, four of Barbarossa's men—complete with big guns slung across their backs—and I, were already in the saddle and a good two miles from the camp-site before golden winter sunlight topped the peaks and exploded through every chink in the fast-moving clouds. The sudden whiteness of the snow made it hurt to look, but the sun's illusional warmth helped me to imagine it cut the bitter wind that was roaring through the tree tops, whipping the thin clouds into foamy wisps, and frosting the breath on my veil into crystals.

In spite of the deep snow at this elevation, we had made good time, stopping in Khenifra yesterday afternoon just long enough to unload, pack the horses, and discuss strategies and directions with Ali's 'cousin.' . . . With *all* of his village 'cousins.'

Everyone in sight had an opinion as to which trail to follow. My grasp of the Tamazight dialect is very slight so I missed most of the discussion. Dick, however, is proficient, and translated some of it for me.

In the end, something the theretofore silent Abu Talib whispered to Ali ended the debate, and in short order we were on our way into the rocky oak and pine woods. When darkness fell yesterday afternoon, we were well along an ancient shepherd's track that switched back dizzily up the mountain's flank.

I'd never gone up this particularly obscure trace, but from what I remembered from my medical teams visits to groups of Berbers dotting these heights, I had to agree with Ali: heading straight up and over the peak would prove to be the shortest route to Imilchil. That high village inexplicably seemed to be Mendoza's next destination.

Imilchil squats defiantly on a mile-high lake plateau surrounded by even taller rocky pinnacles. Life is rigorous. Vegetation is sparse. The sheep-herding clans clinging to existence up there are secretive, obstinate about change, and largely unknown to outsiders.

With many men packing heavy equipment and Polisario food supplies, the Volcares had been forced to follow the wider, but longer market trail over Djebel Masker, farther north than this one. Ali's 'cousin' had assured us that was the Volcares' only choice since they wished to avoid the well-traveled paved pass through Midelt.

My small, dappled mare was gentle, and a steady climber. Calmly following single-file behind Ali, then Sami, Tleta picked her way daintily upward along the hoof-wide path, causing my heart to lurch only when she unavoidably slipped on slick rocks hidden beneath the crust of snow. Here in the sloping, rugged terrain shielded by trees, the snow wasn't as deep as below.

As the hours wore on, the sun did warm the air enough to cause some frozen patches to melt. I discarded my woolen topper and swiveled in my seat to stuff it behind the elaborate, oversized saddle.

Though Dick was directly behind me, my backward glance caught the hooded stare of Kef Rala. His unwavering scrutiny gave me a new type of chill, but I left my coat as planned, and turned around again as casually as I could.

Perhaps my nonchalance would show him I was unconcerned and unafraid of him, but I could still feel his calculating gaze boring a hole between my shoulder blades.

I tried to concentrate on any verse I could remember. This would be a very good time for a word from the Lord, and prayer. But my errant memory was empty. I scolded myself. This time when I get home, I will really stick with a serious program of memorization so that in situations like this . . . this . . . .

What *was* Mendoza doing? If headed for the oasis at Taouz (which made sense, due east of Taouz is the shortest way out of Morocco and into Algeria) why would he now drop so far south into the most rugged High Atlas around Imilchil?

I could see that heading directly over the savage high country during a harsh winter was an effective way to flush out any tail, as well as to lose one. This, after all, was the very wilderness that proved impossible for past invaders to conquer, much less to hold. So even today, except to visit resort areas, very few plain-dwellers—including the national *Sûreté*—venture off the highways into the rugged Atlas. With their craving for privacy, native guides are likely to be as wild and unreliable as the terrain.

So there is no police force out here, to speak of, other than the Royal Moroccan army's ski patrol schussing around the ski slopes in their fancy uniforms. They work mainly with frostbitten tourists.

The superstitious *Ait Addidou* tribe of Imilchil would be suspicious of outsiders like Mendoza and his large entourage. How could his Volcares have an 'in' with back country Berbers who had no interest in any but local politics?

Tleta stumbled and buckled slightly under me. Snapped out of my unpleasant ruminations, I grabbed her mane in alarm, but kept my seat.

"Are you all right, Eve?" Dick kept his voice low. The wind had died down. The only other sounds were the swishing of horse hooves through the snow and the creak of leather saddles.

I glanced over my shoulder with a smile. "I'm fine . . . just wasn't paying attention."

Kef Rala, however, was still paying attention.

I gripped the reins firmly and patted the little mare's neck, giving soft encouragements. A fragment from the Psalms—the one Dick quoted—flashed across my memory:

In God I have put my trust, I shall not be afraid,
What can man do to me?

*Only what you allow, Father. I ask for your protection—for Shay and myself. Please protect and preserve Joe, J.D., Ben, Kit, and Alyssa at home. I miss them so much. Bring us together again . . . .*

Then came:

Thou art my hiding place;
Thou dost preserve me from trouble;
Thou dost surround me with songs of deliverance.

There was a tune with that one. I sang it quietly to myself.

## 16

Over the next rise, the sparse lights of Imilchil twinkled faintly against the enveloping winter darkness.

There wasn't much else to see. I slithered down from my lookout on the ledge overhanging the small basin where we set up camp.

This time of year, night comes early to the mountains. As I brushed icy grit off the front of my jacket, I wondered how many more minutes of light Morocco gets than we do at home, since this is much closer to the equator and Washington is so far north. Of course, by January, even in winter-weary Washington, days are again growing ever-so-slowly longer in anticipation of spring.

I rejoined the men round the fire and accepted a chunk of *kesrah* and a cup of stew they called *tajin*. The hot copper mug felt good on my freezing fingers. The food smelled delicious, and I was hungry, but I was also suddenly weary. So many unused riding muscles ached all at once, that it seemed like too great an effort to chew and swallow.

We kept four spoiled fat horses on our own acreage. The girls and I love to ride. But with winter, and one thing or another, I hadn't been on horseback for months, and my aging body didn't appreciate being reintroduced to the saddle with a daylong marathon.

The faces of my companions reflected my own exhaustion. All except the two nomads. The taciturn black man and his leather-skinned comrade registered no emotion, no hint of the thoughts beyond their wary, now-averted eyes. Having finished their meal, they were curled in their dark robes. Each was tightly folded into himself, aloof from the rest of us.

We had kept pushing up the trail long after full darkness descended. As the gloom deepened, Ali broke out strong battery-powered lanterns, one for himself and one for the rear man. The rest of us had to leave it to our mounts to continue following the horse rump directly in front of his or her nose.

Our leader's determination to reach the Imilchil plateau before Mendoza was contagious. Throughout the day I had begun to see it in the tense set of Sami's shoulders, and in the furrow between Dick's brows.

And we'd done it. By laboring persistently up the mountain's side on that nearly invisible sheep track, we had arrived before the bad guys.

As Sami and I arranged the camp in this sheltered rock bowl a mile or so away from the main village, Ali and Dick had taken the other men on a scouting party. They skirted the highland to confirm that the Volcares had not yet reached the Imilchil plateau.

Now, back at the fire, Sami spoke up.

"*Akbar*, what do we do when the Volcares arrive?" he asked his master expectantly, giving voice to my own questions. We were all blindly trusting in Ali's plan.

"Not tonight, *Abd-el-Ali*, tired men do not make wise decisions, nor remember orders well." Ali softened his refusal to answer by giving Sami the honorary title, 'servant of Ali.'

119

The slender boy wriggled like a petted pup. Whether it was because he'd been indirectly included among the men, or was content with the subtle endearment, Sami fell into an amenable silence.

"Do you have a plan, Ali?" I was reminded many times during those long hours straddling Tleta that I'd also willing-ly followed Ali into this inevitable showdown, trusting his judgement. I'd tacitly agreed not to complain, but nothing had been said about being informed.

"*Madame* must not worry herself. This is man's work. You will stay in camp until we bring your friend back to you—when the time is right.

"We must sleep now," Ali continued, standing and stretch-ing. "Salim. Ahmed. You two take the first watch. Be alert for the first sign of our enemies. They, too, may travel through the darkness to camp here."

The men—with the exception of the motionless nomads—all rose and drifted away from the fire in search of their sleeping mats, leaving their mugs and utensils on the ground.

I was too stunned to move. Ali's abrupt dismissal had hit me like a physical blow.

I should have remembered! But I was taken in by Ali's veneer of urbane acceptance about my participation in this venture. He wouldn't be any different than the other young, unmarried males in Muslim countries. He just wasn't pre-pared to deal with me as a friend, a co-worker, or even as a human being that (barring gender) was like himself.

No. I was Woman: mysterious, desirable for certain pur-poses, largely forbidden, and wholly inferior. This culture shocked me all right.

Of course, I had threatened his cultural sensibilities, too. As we all do when culture-shocked, Ali had simply scurried back into the comfortable familiarity of ingrained habits—especially with other men looking on. I should have recog-nized his reversion coming on by slow degrees. It paralleled our journey back up into this wilderness. It accompanied the mounting pressure we'd all felt since leaving Marrakesh.

Dick lingered to help pick up the abandoned dinner utensils, which had, I realized with another jolt, been left for me to clean.

Everyone in my household shares cooking and cleaning chores—male and female. I have often blessed Naomi (which, over the years grandchildren have changed to 'Nomi'), my mother-in-*love*, for teaching her farm sons domestic skills. Not being bred myself to be a wife and mommy, we would never have survived the earliest years of family life without Joe's culinary and housekeeping abilities.

Before Ali sauntered too far away from the fire ring, Dick jumped into the breach. Copper cups still in hand, he stepped closer to our leader, and raised his voice.

"I would like to know, Ali. *Do* you have a plan?"

Ali turned. "Of course. I have a very good plan," he answered curtly. "Surprise is my main weapon. My men and I have experience at such things," he added as though challenging Dick to meet his standard.

"But," he continued in a condescending tone, "it is also most likely we will have all of tomorrow to prepare. Let us sleep now so we will be strong and cunning in the fight." His black eyes gleamed in the glow from the dying flames. "Good night." Ali stalked away.

By the light of a lantern, I saw him squat and confer with one of his men near a technical-looking box that I took to be some sort of radio.

He still had communication with the outside, then. With whom? Barbarossa? Bennani? Surely not Aziz?

Once the dishes were wiped as clean as we could get them with snow and rags, I thanked Dick, said goodnight, took my flashlight, and slogged through the wet slush toward my designated sleeping quarters at the bottom of the rock ledge.

As I trudged alone into the darkness, Joe's words of warning came back to me. What if Ali *had* brought us—me—here to sell to Mendoza. He was acting strangely. Maybe he was contacting the terrorist leader right now and arranging a meeting time.

*"Madame! Madame!"* Sami's hushed call broke into my anxious musings.

Catching Sami in my flashlight beam, I could see that his arms were straining to enfold something soft and awkward.

"Is this where *Madame* wishes to settle?" he asked formally. You would have thought he'd grown up the son of a concierge instead of an Islamic scholar. Sami was eagerly trying on new identities as rapidly as my Ben. Suddenly, it cheered me to realize that Ben felt free enough to experiment with life's many choices while he was still at home. Stifled for fourteen years, Sami was just now reveling in his new-found liberty.

I nodded. I'd already pitched my tiny tent under the rock shelf in the most likely level spot. With his Saint Bernard puppy feet, Sami gallantly whisked away what snow had drifted in around it. Then—*voila!*—out of the thin mountain air he unfurled one, then two magic carpets.

Actually, they were hanging tapestries woven in dark, rich colors. Rolled inside were the collapsible frames that raised them into instant partitions. Their sudden, practically airborne appearance seemed to my overtired mind like the flying rugs of *Arabian Nights.* And where they'd been stashed among all the supplies and ammunition loaded onto two pack animals, I'll never know.

As Sami stood back to admire his handiwork, I commented on his manifest happiness.

"Oh, I have been wanting to tell *Madame*! Much happened for me last night after you retired," he gushed eagerly.

"You must know, I had to explain my dishonor—my family's shame in this matter—to the *ackbar.* After I tell, he goes to the CB—the radio? He makes a call.

"Oh, *Madame*! Through this, M. Bakkali tells his man, 'Go to the home of the Oukfir relative living in the hills near the *moussem* bridge of Imi N'Ifri,'" Sami said, shivering.

*Moussems* are early pilgrimages to local shrines (*koubbas*).

The believers go each year to honor dead local saints, called *marabouts*. These short trips are the next best thing to the required *hadj* to Mecca.

The evil rites of the hillfolk in the Imi N'Ifri area, where hundreds of shrieking crows roost along the dank river tunnel, made a shiver pass down my spine too.

"When my father sends Malika to the country, this old uncle by the river of crows was the first one in my mind."

Smiling widely, he continued, "Tonight, I am assured, she was there, as I thought.

"Also, I am told, *M.* Bakkali's man paid to my relative a fine price for my sister. Now he is taking her to be with *les Madames* and *Mademoiselles* Moffat and Foster at Barbarossa's *dar* in Fez. My father will never find her there. She will be safe until I return from this pursuit."

He drew his wiry frame straight up to its full height and raised his chin. I glimpsed in his bearing, and his next words, the man he was becoming.

"I shall serve the *Monsieur*—my *akbar*—for the rest of my life if that is what it takes to pay back, not only the bride price of *dirhams* and animals, but also his kindness to us."

Then, as quickly as it appeared, the maturity evaporated, and Sami performed a theatrical, hand-waving *salaam*. "May Allah bless you greatly for bringing *M.* Bakkali to help us and *Mlle.* O'Shea."

Not waiting for any response, he bowed himself away, turned, and loped back over the snowy ground to his hero.

I crawled into my little shelter behind the woven walls, and burrowed deep in the mummy bag with a grateful sigh. I was too drained to waste any more time being angry, curious, or afraid.

I should have been too tired to dream. But from wherever Joe lives inside my heart or inside my soul, he crept out over the barriers I'd put up the last two days to shut him out. Joe came to me in one of the most memorable dreams I've ever had. And one of the worst.

I was sitting at a window table in the cafeteria at Saint Camillus. At 800 beds, it's the largest hospital in Eastern Washington. St. Cami perches impressively atop a steep hill in downtown Kamas Falls, and the view from the dining room is one of the best in town.

Joe and I often arrange to meet there to begin our dates. It's not as bad as one might think. Although a busman's holiday of sorts, not only does the decor approach that of a legitimate three star restaurant, the food is really good. And it's cheaper than a regular restaurant.

With two large and two small hospitals, Kamas Falls is the medical hub of the tri-state area. Even Canadians hop the border for treatment.

So the Kamas Falls medical centers compete for business in every way possible—cafeteria cuisine, and menu prices, were two of them.

I turned away from the city lights to see my husband striding across the massive room. He was wearing his favorite red plaid shirt, jeans, and well-worn, but polished, cowboy boots.

Joe smiled his crooked, rogue's smile when he caught me watching him. His angular face, with its twice-broken nose and pleasant scar curved under the left eye, was amiable and intriguing.

Even now, the sudden sight of him clutches my breath and registers a bolt of heat to my mid-section like it did—more than it did—when I first met him.

Dr. Joseph Daniels is a lean, tanned tower of a man who, at six-four, moves with compact, muscular grace. His powerful shoulders, gained from years of outdoor work and varsity athletics, lead down to large, callused, but surprisingly gentle hands. Slim hips anchor two impossibly long legs.

But the feature that reaches out to capture and hold your attention is his eyes. They are literally turquoise, shot with icy white streaks so vivid they dance with incandescence. Even the shock of raven hair that is forever threatening to fall into them cannot diminish their ability to look directly

124

into your soul. But when he breaks out his lopsided grin, complete with one great dimple under the scar, most people don't seem to mind—only those with something to hide.

My dream man leisurely strolled the rest of the distance to the table. With a wink, he said, "May I have this dance?," and held out a big, rough paw.

We waltzed around the floor, and, as things do in dreams, the tables melted away.

I looked down and discovered I was wearing a lacy white ball gown complete with bridal veil. Joe's jeans and old boots had given way to a crisp black tuxedo and a formal black tie. I knew this was just after our wedding, though the real event was a happy, impoverished affair that didn't include fancy Viennese frocks.

My heart was soaring with the passionate music and the feel of Joe's strong arms around me. I looked up and was caught by the glow in those fabulous eyes. Just before our lips could touch, I heard children laughing, and felt small hands tugging at my full skirts.

Joe and I were surrounded by our offspring—also elaborately attired and wanting to join in the dance. Each of them were such precious blessings. The overflow of love and gratitude within me as I looked at them became an exquisite ache I would willingly carry all of my days.

With happy tears, I knelt down and gathered them in my arms, hungrily kissing all their cool, smooth faces. Since this was a dream, even J.D. and Ben didn't seem to mind.

"Lyndy! Don't be such a stupid fool!" Mother's strident command shattered the tender moment.

The children stiffened and shrank away in fear until they disappeared into the deep shadows at the edges of the room.

I rose to face my mother who was staring angrily at me. The form of my father stood silently beside her, an empty husk.

They, too, were attired formally in their best Rodeo Drive designer originals—sophisticated, polished, brittle. But something was wrong with their faces, especially my mother's face. Something was radiating out of her eyes that caused me physical pain.

A scathing lecture was bursting from her mouth, but her tongue seemed to be so jagged, it was difficult to make out the words. I was fascinated by that odd tongue flicking in and out as she berated me.

"I gave you everything . . . everything! *SSSsss* . . . . Issss thissss how you repay me? You could make ssssomething of yourssssself with all the advantagessss I never had.

"But, no! You turn down good offerssss. Real offerssss! And turn your nosssse up at the interesssst of all the right boyssss. I had to claw my way up . . . but are you sssssmart enough to do that? To ussssse . . . ."

The hissing tirade broke off when Joe stepped between my parents and me. Behind the shield of his body, I peered around at the two of them. But the words began again and kept flowing out and around him to hurt me.

My parents began to move toward us, to bear down on Joe and I. I could see then that my father had no face at all. There was just a blank stretch of dead white skin where eyes, nose and mouth should be. That lifeless non-face was even more frightening than the hate-twisted maw of my mother's.

Suddenly, Mother shrieked and flew at Joe, clawing at him with her curved red talons. Locked in a deadly struggle they rolled across the floor and were lost in the darkness.

My faceless father was coming for me. As his stiff, pale fingers brushed my skin, I ducked his grasp with a scream and ran outside into barren hills. It was bleak and piercingly cold. My lovely dress was in shreds. I was lost and utterly alone.

Then, from far in the distance, I heard Joe's voice calling my name.

"Eve, where are you? I'm coming, darling. Don't be afraid."

"Joe? . . . Joe, I'm over here in the hills."

I woke up drenched in sweat, with Joe's name still on my lips. Dizzy, disoriented and trembling, I struggled to catch my breath. Ducking so I wouldn't uproot my low-slung shelter, I slid into an angled sitting position, and worked the sleeping bag over my exposed shoulders. Just over my head, a freezing sleet was pelting the tent.

Hugging knees to my chest, I rested my head on them until the worst of the throbbing began to fade. The nightmare terrors receded along with the headache.

It was dawn—Tuesday morning—a week since I had received the call.

# 17

Dawn's sleet changed to a steady snowfall hurled side-ways by gusty crosswinds. In spite of the blustering weather, the whole of that unlovely Tuesday was spent in feverish preparations and short scouting trips.

I cleaned and loaded guns, kept snowdrifts swept out of the fire, did a little cooking, but basically stayed out of the men's way. I stamped around a great deal trying to keep my fingers and toes from freezing solid.

If fuming didn't keep me warm, it at least took my mind off the cold. I was parked on the bench with no chance to play, and I didn't much like the feeling of being a bench warmer.

Looking for Shay had been my idea all along. And if it weren't for me, Ali wouldn't have been called in to help. Help! He'd walked in and taken over.

I had plenty of time to pray. But I wasn't much in the mood. I prefer action, and with each passing minute, the showdown was coming closer. Inside, I was coiled to spring, but the lid had been firmly put on my basket. I understood how the snake charmers' cobras felt. Frustrated.

Wind-chapped and weary, Dick came back from a morning survey of the plateau. He joined me under my ledge sometime after the sketchy mid-day meal of dried mutton and crackers. Sheltered here from the swirling snow, in deference to his protesting sitting muscles, he carefully planted his hefty frame on a handy rock, and asked if we couldn't read the Word together and pray.

My own reluctance shocked me with a stab of shame. I suddenly recalled other times God had sidelined me until I took the essential action of prayer. Those were times I'd sworn to myself I'd never again forget to wait on God prayerfully—to not flail around on my own power.

So, with ungraciously mixed feelings—I wasn't ready to stop being mad just yet—I looked at the Bible with the missionary.

A little repentant, I agreed with him while he asked God for protection and guidance.

"Lord, help us rescue Shay successfully. Please let her escape without any loss of life on either side. Without any violence at all, if possible, Father. Open the way for us," he prayed.

Then, we prayed for our adversaries. At the moment, it was easier than praying for some of my friends. But even at that, I have to admit, it was one of those: "Make-me-willing-to-be-willing-to-love-them-as-You-do" prayers.

A shout over at the firepit caught our attention.

Dick and I topped off our requests with quick "Amens," and scurried through the driving whiteness to join the men listening to Ali's and Sami's report.

The two had spotted the Volcares—ten men, plus one smaller rider being led through the blinding storm. Shay! The group was, they said, slogging upward through the snow drifts clogging the market trail.

"They will reach the plain here by nightfall," Sami estimated cheerfully. He was looking forward to a fight.

"Your friend, the *mademoiselle*, was sitting upright on her own horse," Ali said. "Her head was bent down because of the snow, but her manner was alert enough, not swaying or weak. I think she has not been drugged very much.

"Her hands and legs were tied to the saddle, but that is a good sign. Her captors think she will still try to escape," Ali reported to me, shouting against the roar of the wind. "She was wrapped warmly against the cold," he added gently.

In that instant, I forgave every bit of his stupid macho behavior. Ali cared the best he could. He cared enough to try to put my mind at ease.

"We will pray. We will eat." Ali rose as he made these pronouncements. "Then, *M.* Foster," he yelled over his shoulder as he made his way toward his small tent snapping in the wind, "I will tell you my plan."

Ali joined his men in their ablutions—using snow to cleanse hands and faces. Then they began their mid-day prayers facing Mecca, laying prayer mats on top of the packed snow near the fire. Today they were very devout at their series of prayers. Just as we had been.

Sami, however, squatted down near Dick and I by the fire, turning his back on the Islamic ritual taking place.

The two dark nomads were nowhere to be seen. As desert dwellers, perhaps they sought to get in out of the cold. Just like spies.


The winds died down with the waning afternoon light.

Our entire party was packed and ready to move at a moment's notice, each with our individual marching orders.

Just as the short winter dusk swallowed the last natural illumination, one of Ali's burly henchmen came galloping recklessly into camp at breakneck speed, splattering snow as he skidded to a spectacular stop by the fire.

From his rapid-fire account, I caught the words, "camp," "rocks something . . .", and a phrase about "the lake."

Imilchil is dotted with innumerable small, clear pools. But

the plain's two largest lakes are legendary characters.

In close proximity, but never touching, Tislit, the female, and Isli, the male, are said to be separated lovers betrothed since the beginning of time. They were doomed by a wicked somebody to long for each other eternally, since the gap between will never be spanned.

The bowl in which we had camped lay just above the north end of Tislit. Perhaps that's why my ledge, closest to the lake, was considered the woman's quarter.

After this last storm, the grieving and treacherous lady lake looked only like a broad, smooth flatland of unmarred snow. But one could never assume that, even at this time of year, her heart would be frozen solid. Fortunately, Dick had done some summer fishing up here and the locals had warned him about the hidden winter danger.

As soon as the scout finished his report, the murmuring men crouched together round the dwindling fire to receive final instructions.

Their complement was restored. Kef Rala and Abu Talib had rematerialized sometime near the end of the afternoon with sinister curved scimitars at their sides, and efficient automatic rifles strapped on their backs.

Once, after they returned, I'd caught Ali in a furtive study of Kef Rala that made me wonder how much he really trusted his own mercenary guides.

I already had my assignment, and had been dismissed to wait at the edge of the darkness with the horses.

It was easier to be obedient now that we were so close to Shay. I was thinking of her, not myself. It helped also that my curiosity had been satisfied by Dick, who'd passed Ali's plan on to me.

Ali intended to place his men strategically around the perimeters of the terrorist camp and raid Shay's quarters himself while the Volcares were sleeping. Although closely matched in numbers, Ali didn't want to have an outright battle with the combat-trained, quasi-military group if he could avoid it. But, Dick reported with chagrin, my old friend had

131

no qualms about slitting throats during a sneak attack.

Dick had argued with him against the need for killing, except for self-defense. Ali argued back that it would "defend many selves" by getting in and away cleanly. Plus, he'd reasoned, when the shift changed, and the dead guards were discovered, there would be fewer men to come after us. Neither man had convinced the other, but, in Marrakesh, Dick had agreed to follow Ali's direction, and now he would back him up. Dick would be Ali's lookout. "Praying all the time the guard will be sound asleep!" Dick had muttered to me.

The men around the fire broke their huddle. They stood up.

"Allah promises to help those who fight in His way!" Even though speaking quietly, Ali's voice rang with authority as he spoke the invocation in Arabic.

"In the name of Allah! By the name of the Prophet!" chanted the men together.

Gooseflesh prickled my arms, but not because of the temperature. Those were ancient battle cries of Muslim warriors. They were invoking Allah's power—giving him the glory.

With booted feet they aggressively stomped the embers of the dying fire. Horses were mounted with tense quickness. The point men lit our path with dim lanterns. Thus, single file, we left camp, heading east. Our perceptive mounts were prancing, jingling harnesses, and snorting smoke into the still, crisp air.

Sami and I brought up the rear. My assignment was to lag behind, out of the way. A sullen Sami had been ordered to keep an eye on me. We were to conceal ourselves and be ready to bolt down a nearby rough *piste* that headed back toward Khenifra as soon as our warriors returned with their prize.

Most of the dirt *pistes* are navigable by a sturdy car in the summer, so this one should afford us an easier way down than the trace that brought us up, if it wasn't totally blocked by the last snowfall.

That hadn't worried Ali. It just so happened that his Khenifra "cousin," whom he'd alerted by shortwave, earned income during the winter months with his snowplow equipment. If Cousin did his job, we ought to make good time downhill. At least half way downhill.

After the rescue, our men were to ride off in every direction to confuse the Volcares. Ali, bringing Shay, was to lead Sami and I down the road until we met his cousin, plowing his way up to meet us. Cousin's son was going to be following his Dad in our land rover, in which we'd beat it back to Fez at top speed. Hopefully, the highway crews would be as diligent as Ali's enigmatic relatives were supposed to be.

I was so busy reviewing the plans, I wasn't prepared when the man in front of me reined in his stallion abruptly. I almost rearended him.

The man crooked his neck back and whispered hoarsely in gruff English.

"You—the two. Wait here."

Then he jabbed at the air with his fingers, indicating Sami and I and the road. His orders obeyed, he turned and galloped off after the others.

The wind was rising again and I was grateful for it. It covered the sounds of horsemen stealing up to the outskirts of the terrorist camp. The wind had also made it difficult to understand the man's words to Sami and me. Had he told us to wait here—or go further?

The blowing gusts concealed the sound of two more horses following the group that continued on ahead.

My assignment was to stay behind and be ready. I would do both—a little closer.

## 18

There wasn't much vegetation for cover, so Sami and I tethered our well-mannered horses to the twisted branches of a bush and walked the last mile. Or rather, we waded, slow motion, through the churned up knee-deep accumulation of powdery snow.

Sweaty inside my woolens after that exercise at this altitude, I was relieved when the raw wind was deflected by a rock formation as we reached the far side of Lake Tislit.

"Get down!" I grabbed for Sami, and switched off the flashlight.

As my eyes adjusted to the darkness, I could clearly make out what I thought I'd seen—a large campfire, with an attentive bevy of tents nesting in a hollow. The flat hollow was tucked up against the foot of a mountain peak rising thousands of feet into the clearing night sky.

I knew this place. Long ago, our clinic team set up shop one hot August week on this same high lake plain of Tizi N' Tenehet.

The Volcare camp was a good half-mile across the plateau from where we crouched under a clump of stunted scrub pine.

Once Sami spotted the campfire, he developed an annoying tendency to pop up for a better look. Having to pull him down repeatedly, I also tried to get my bearings on a landscape lighted only by stars peering through torn remnants of cloud.

I didn't want to get close enough to be seen by either Ali's men, who must be concealed among the rocks and shadows, or by the Volcares. Every man on both sides were armed and charged for a fight. Any of them might shoot at our unexplained movement. Nor did I want to slither closer to the hidden, nearby lake.

I could just visualize the fitting Falls Review headline: "Local Resident Drowns Under Ice in Darkest Africa!"

No! I shook my head like Kit's Etch-A-Sketch to erase that mental picture. I could fall through the ice at one of our water holes back home any time. Travel is meant to offer novel experiences.

The present situation offered enough troubles to think about. I was back to peering intently through the gnarled pine branches when two things happened simultaneously.

The storm front conclusively blew itself over the mountain tops to die in the desert. With most of the clouds gone, the sliver of a crescent moon and a solid spangle of white stars sharpened the contrast enough for me to distinguish a slender shadow bent low and creeping sideways across the flank of the mountain.

Pulling off a glove, I rummaged for the binoculars in my bag of tricks—my *choukhara*, the big Moroccan leather holdall, worn sideways across the body. My fingers bumped against the small Smith and Wesson resting at the bottom. Its touch of steel was cold and deadly. I winced at the reminder, and quickly groped in another corner of the pouch.

"What can you see, *Madame?*" asked Sami, looking pointedly

135

at the field glasses and avidly flexing his hands. I was surprised his burning curiosity didn't thaw the snow around him. At least the inquisitiveness melted his sullenness at being left behind. It also seemed to have replaced his reluctance to follow this strange female across the dangerous highlands—against his master's orders.

"I think it's your *ackbar*. There—on the mountainside." He snatched the glasses as soon as I offered them. As he squinted at the stealthy speck, I suggested, "Lets get closer. We can still get back to the trail head in plenty of time."

Bending over at the waist made it awkward, but I waded straight out onto the snowy plain toward the beacon of firelight. Sami enthusiastically plunged behind me. I was confident that Tislit lay off to our right. I hoped Dick and Ali's men remembered where she was.

After drudging another half-mile, often on hands and knees, and panting in the thin air, we stopped to take a closer look at the Volcares' camp.

Focusing the binoculars, I scanned anxiously, but could no longer see the deliberate, moving form on the mountainside.

Without warning, a piercing howl sliced the stillness and shattered the heavy silence. It was followed by the shrill yodeling cries of charging Berber horsemen and rounds of gunfire.

At the first scream, I dropped the field glasses. Pulling Sami down flat beside me into the snow, I wiped off the lenses as best I could with my wet sleeve.

We didn't need them to see the disaster happen.

Portable floodlights came on in every corner of the Volcare encampment, until a full square mile of Tizi N' Tenehet was brighter than day. Armed Volcares on horseback appeared from nowhere. Most carried powerful handheld spotlights aimed outward beyond the boundary of the larger illumination.

Then, a turbaned figure, waving his rifle overhead, galloped wildly down the mountain into the blazing camp, and

136

pulled his stallion up short in front of a tent. In one fluid movement, Kef Rala leaped off his mount and swept aside the tent flap.

Ali, hands clasped on top of his head, stumbled back out through the opening seconds later, prodded by the shaft of the Touareg's rifle. With one hand holding the weapon to Ali's head, Kef Rala used the other to drag Shay into the light by jerking the fingers he'd twisted into her short red hair.

A stubby little man in olive drab fatigues, complete with cap and beard like a stunted Fidel Castro, emerged from the tent nearest the fire. He spoke briefly to Kef Rala, who inclined his head in acknowledgement, then wrenched Shay to the ground, and impassively held her there.

At the little man's order, two more of his henchmen, dressed in the efficient black jumpsuit of the Volcares, dismounted and pinned Ali's arms, while Mendoza began to batter my Moroccan friend with his fists. Mendoza's black leather gloves were probably adorned with the ever popular triangular metal studs. I saw Ali's knees buckle.

*Dear God, we were so close. What can be done now?*

In swift answer to prayer, another shadow caught my eye as it careened down the rubbly slope behind the tragic scene. From the uniquely magnificent horse, and the rider's skill, it had to be Abu Talib.

Standing in his tasseled stirrups, the second nomad was firing two of those condensed machine guns Ali's men called Uzis. With one in each hand, Abu Talib was scattering the mounted terrorists, and sending snowy sprays of rock and gravel pinging all around Mendoza's feet.

Taken by surprise, Mendoza's party froze in their brutal tableau for a few seconds. Then, Kef Rala hurled Shay across the snow and drew his own weapon on the charging black fury.

"Look ou—" Automatically, I started to call out a warning, when I became aware that Sami was tugging my pant leg and emitting guttural moans. I realized I'd been on my feet and moving forward for some time. The boy had been clinging to my ankles, and, unaware, I'd been dragging his body through the slush.

"They will find us! They have lights. We must run! Please *Madame*, our orders . . . . We must leave from here!"

I turned back to answer his pleas when three more automatic blasts burped in quick succession. I swung round to see Kef Rala stiffen and sprawl backwards in the snow. Mendoza, too, slumped down. Ali lurched to his feet and began to wrestle one of the guards for his gun. The second soldier was taking aim on the mounted warrior swooping straight at him. The sounds of more distant gunfire reverberated through the darkness outside the floodlit camp.

Shay, with characteristic spunk, and no sense of direction, picked up the entangling folds of her *djellaba* and began to sprint—or the closest approximation one can manage in the snow. She was running southward.

"Not that way, Shay! The lake . . . !" I cried.

Eluding Sami's grip, I stumbled forward on frozen feet, slushing through the melting snowpack as fast as I could.

"No! No! The Volcares, *Madame!*" Sami shouted behind me.

Without breaking stride, I shouted back over my shoulder. Silence no longer mattered. "You go straight back the way we came. Get down the *piste* and meet Ali's cousin. Call Doctor Dawson-Rhys in Fez. Bring help!"

Hearing no response, I stopped long enough to turn around. My vision was blurry from the spectacular brilliance in front of me. I could barely see Sami in the gentler moonlight. The boy was rooted to the same spot I left.

"Do what I say, Sami! Call Dr. Dawson-Rhys. Go, now!"

I think he moved his head. Whether in bewilderment, or in agreement, I'm not sure. In any case, his shadow bent over in a slight bow, turned tail, and bounded back through the slush toward the horses.

"Have the doctor call my husband," I called as an afterthought.

I set out once more on my diagonal course, hoping to intersect Shay before she hit the shore of the invisible lake. Pushing through the knee-deep thaw was exhausting work. I was again sweating uncomfortably inside my wet woolens but losing all normal sensation in my frigid extremities. Inside the soft leather boots, my feet clunked like chunks of petrified wood.

With fatigue and anxiety, time was distorted. The landscape around me looked smeared like a surrealistic painting. Soon it seemed I'd been stumbling forward forever through this dim funhouse equipped with strobe lights and fake explosions echoing screams. Following the pace of my own steady panting, I put one foot in front of the other like an automaton.

Then I saw her. Down a slight slope, I could make out a small figure silhouetted against a smooth expanse of alabaster. She was still moving fast—but with a jerky lunge that showed she was tiring.

I peeled the moist scarf and muffler away from my face. I was running now. "Shay. Stop!" I shouted, waving the scarf with my arms.

She hadn't heard.

I wiped my streaming nose on my coarse sleeve and tried again.

"Shay! It's me, Eve. You're out on the lake. Stop!"

I could see the creamy oval of her face as she turned it toward me. At that distance, I probably only imagined her eyes widening in surprise.

"Eve?" Shay's voice carried across the distance to me. I didn't realize how quiet it had become on the plateau. "Is that really you?"

"It's me! It's Eve. I'm really here!" I kept screaming and running and waving.

Distinguishing my shape from the mottled surroundings, she turned, picked up the hem of her robe, and began to move in my direction while waving her other arm over her head in joyous abandon.

Somehow she recognized me. Maybe the moon lit it up, or maybe I could just feel her smile, but I knew she had a big one, and it certainly matched mine.

Then Shay vanished.

Stunned, I stopped and stared for a few precious seconds at the sudden gaping hole in the snow before my tired mind could comprehend what had happened.

Weighed down by yards of water-logged material, Shay would drown within minutes in Tislit's freezing waters.

I began to strip off my outer layers, hardly aware of the activity around me. I hit the icy water with a quick, nonverbal prayer like the one Peter gave when he began to sink beneath the waves: *Lord, save me! . . . No, save us. Bring us back to walk on the surface, too.*

Kicking downward like I'd learned in my 'Y' lessons, I tried to keep my eyes open against the stabbing cold. For some reason there was quite a bit of murky light shining down here beneath the thin ice. Mercifully, on my first sweeping dive, my numb fingers fumbled into something hard with softer tendrils around it. Shay's head.

Fighting down the lengths of snarling wool, I struggled to make my unresponsive hands cup her chin. I winced as I had to pull at her poor scalp like Kef Rala had done earlier.

The billowing folds of her heavy *djellaba* swirled and pulled around us, but they had probably trapped enough air to slow her original descent instead of sinking her straight to the bottom.

I finally managed to grapple a hold under her arms and, with the residue of my strength, kicked upward toward the light.

The winter air bit at my face as we broke the surface. I gasped in huge lungfulls of the glorious stuff. But my moment of relief was short-lived.

There were rough hands and voices everywhere. I was hauled up and dumped face-down on the snowy shore. A stiff covering was tossed over me.

In the few minutes I lay there, shivering must have warmed my brain back to thinking temperature. The notion that appeared there chilled me more than the wintry weather.

I tried to free my eyelids from the ice crystals fusing the lashes together. Slowly peeling a corner of the canvas tarp off my face, I raised my shoulders with shaky arms and turned my head—to find myself squinting into the business end of a very large gun.

Lit by the intermittent beams of unnaturally bright flashlights, I followed the barrel upward until I found a mean, superior smile slicing across an appropriately ugly mug. If any face deserved that description, it was this Maroc's. His visage looked exactly like Joe's beloved coffee cup at home: round, thick, stained brown, and covered with cracks.

"Bring the tall one over here."

Mug and his helper gouged long fingers into my armpits and dragged me farther up the bank. They forced me to teeth-chattering attention in front of the short Spaniard wearing the miniature set of Castro's clothes.

I had the shakes so bad it was hard to concentrate, but I forced myself to swallow the dangerous giggle that rose in my throat. Though his appearance approached caricature, the malevolent fanaticism apparent in the man's face was no joke.

The terrorist *ulama*, Mendoza, was a deadly serious fat man of fifty. Not standing over five-two, his compact intensity was punctuated by a greasy black beard and protuberant dark eyes. Despite the frigid air, he was sweating profusely. Maybe that was a by-product of the bloody gash ripped across the upper-left hand shoulder of his tunic. Mendoza *did* hold that arm crooked inward—like Napoleon.

"So," the little man said, "your crude heroics have saved our merchandise and doubled our inventory at the same time." He spoke in flawless English. A well-educated crazy man.

Mendoza reached up with his chubby right hand and used

one of its sausage-like appendages to finger my crystallized hair. "A blonde? General al-Qadim will be most pleased."

I actually growled and snapped my neck backward to avoid his touch.

The Volcares leader barked shortly, then winced. Catching me off guard, he slapped my face for his pain. "And proud too, like the redhead?" he challenged.

I'd been distracted by the guerrilla behind Mendoza who was draping Shay's limp body over a horse's back. They hadn't thrown her back in the lake, so she must only be unconscious, not dead. Mendoza's next words confirmed that.

"You both will bring a high price." The *ulama* smacked his puffy lips. "A very sweet deal indeed!"

## 19

The stable was close and fetid with the smell of rotting straw and the presence of its four-legged inhabitants. But, being half underground, with thick rock walls and a heavy wooden door—a locked and guarded door—at least our shared pen was relatively warm and dry.

The stalls were in the basement of an extended family home built into the slope of a hillside—a common custom in these elevations. We didn't travel very far from the lake, so I assumed this residence was on the outskirts of the village of Imilchil.

The centuries-old stone house was a broad square, dropping three stair-stepped stories down the valley side. Most likely it had been this family's home for generations. The front door and third floor of the residence were flush with the upper mountain path. Above the main entry would be the fourth floor with more sleeping quarters, perhaps an attic, and a long flat roof used as a patio and observation deck in summer. From the front door, wooden stairs descended through the mortared stone maze of rooms, to another full floor with separate spaces for sleeping, family gatherings, food preparation, and storage.

In Berber homes, when not sleeping or outside, men occupy the main room; men always command the largest room in rural homes. Not so bad here, but if a family only shares the two rooms of an apartment-like *ksour*, the males still use the larger cubicle while all the women, children, and animals in the clan make do with the smaller chamber.

The sheep bleated and huddled fretfully in their corner. Shay and I also had several goats and, I think, two horses as roommates.

I appreciated the fact we were still counted among the livestock. However, as long as we were alive, it seems we were on our way to market.

"MMMMmmm . . ." Shay moaned and bumped my arm as she rolled her head back and forth. She began to cough and muttered as though she was trying to come to.

I had her propped up in the outside corner of the back wall where, hopefully, the straw was cleaner. Since Mendoza shut us in here with no light, it was only conjecture that our roomies' droppings would be over on their side of the floor. It gave me comfort to believe that.

"Cough it all out," I said, as, by feel, I sat her up further and thumped her back lightly.

Shay gave two more gurgling hacks, then I could feel warm water gush over my hand supporting her chest. I prayed it was only lake water. Though sticky, it felt too thin to be, nor did it smell like blood. If she'd aspirated much water, infection or pneumonia or both could set in. She really needed to be in a hospital.

"Eve?" Shay gasped. "Are you real?

"I'm really here, Shay. I came to help find you."

We hugged each other for a good long time. That sweet reunion was worth the price.

"I thought I had an hallucination out there on the plain," she sniffed. "I've been thinking a lot about you the last few days."

Shay took a couple of ragged breaths, but sighed with satisfaction. "Thank you. Thank you for coming. I was so scared," she whispered in a small voice. "I've been wanting to talk things over like we used to."

"I know, honey. But you should rest now, we'll have plenty of time to talk," I soothed.

Reclining her back on the pile of hay, I rubbed her arms, trying to allay the shuddering.

"What happened after I got away from those men? How did you find me? Why is it so cold?" She chattered nervously, but her words slurred as the spurt of energy drained away.

"Later. You need to sleep now. When you wake up we'll make up for lost time."

If we were high-priced merchandise, Mendoza wasn't being very careful of his assets. "Useful, but expendable," I grumbled as I warmed her limbs with friction.

I flushed with anger when I thought about those big, strong soldiers of fortune standing around and letting me save their bargaining chip for them. But, this is the part of the world where, in the Polisario "Zone of Insecurity," men force their wives to walk ahead of them on the road to market, while they ride behind on the donkey or camel. That way, if there is a rebel-planted land mine, the woman steps on it first, allowing man, animal, and trading wares to reach the *souk* safely.

The massage seemed to help Shay. The breathing coming out of the darkness was raspy, but regular with the rhythm of sleep. I pushed the soggy leg of her ski pants up to the knee and started in on her right calf. She needed dry, warm clothes and a clean bed.

This treatment isn't totally Muhammed's fault, I allowed as I chafed Shay's skin. He actually improved social conditions and religious equality for females in lands where girl babies were routinely left to die. The Prophet of Islam intended women and the poor to be cared for. He instituted the law of *Nafaqua,* making it a husband's duty to provide the basic necessities of life to his wife, or wives.

Of course, not being married to any of these guys, and being infidels, made us fair game.

Muhammed had prejudices, too, that cropped up in other teachings. Like the *hadith*, or saying, attributed to him: "Ask the opinion of your wives, but always do the opposite!"

So, here in Morocco, in all the Muslim world, in every society; there are people with tendencies for kindness and for evil, for selfishness and for charity.

Without cleansing from Jesus Christ, and without the Holy Spirit's power living inside, our sin nature will always reveal itself to be stronger than the noblest of human impulses. Selfish pride and the misuse of power are the result of a natural, unchanged heart, whether that heart resides in Africa or the Americas.

I shifted over to work on Shay's left leg, and on my logical conclusions.

The revered founder of Islam called women "tillage," and gave males the right to "plow whenever they wished." So sin-filled men in control, with ingrained cultural biases, took that permission, and enhanced it.

As if on cue, the lock chinked, and the stable door creaked open. Two Volcares stood there, one armed and pointing his weapon at us; the other, just past his teens, was gingerly holding a carbide lamp at arm's length. It's sudden white flame stung my eyes. I blinked against the onrush of frosty air and dazzled vision.

Those lanterns are used throughout the Atlas where there is no electricity. Small copper buckets are filled with white flakes of calcium carbide and a wick. Water is added. The chemical reaction gives off acetylene gas which is inflammable. Inflammable and highly explosive.

"*Yallah!* Let's go!" the armed man yelled, motioning with his stumpy Uzi for us to come out.

"She can't walk." I protested. "And she's still wet. She'll freeze outside."

"*Yallah!*" Louder, with the gun waved more insistently.

Maybe they were taking us someplace warm. "*J'ai* . . . um

146

. . . *besoin d'aide*," I faltered, miming carrying motions. "I need help with her."

The lamp-bearer muttered a few phrases in Arabic at Uzi. Light dawned in Uzi's eyes as he took in Shay's unconscious state.

"*Oui*," Lampbearer snapped. He avoided my eyes with something like embarrassment. Were there some feelings of pity left in this young one? I pressed my opportunity as they picked their way across the stable floor.

"*Elle . . . a besoin . . . le docteur. Le docteur?*" I struggled to convey my message to the young terrorist behind the flame as Uzi scooped Shay up in one arm, and flopped her over his shoulder with a grunt. Lampbearer's response to my question was a shove in the ribs with his weapon, and a gruff, "*Zid!* Go on!"

We scrambled up the steep, glassy path around the side of the house. Uzi, with his precarious burden, still managed to poke his gun one-handed at the small of my back. He drove me onto the upper walkway and in the front entrance.

Once inside, we went down age-blackened stairs to the storeroom and kitchen. Stifling smoke and heat mingled with the lingering haze of meals long past. At the stone archway to the cook room itself, Uzi rolled Shay off his back onto the dirt floor, then he and Lampbearer backed away to squat sourly among the heaps of nuts and stacked baskets. Only women ever enter the kitchen.

Four pairs of frightened dark eyes appeared in the doorway. Two, tired and wrinkled by life: the grandmother. Two, quick and keen, but wary: the head wife. And four peeping out shyly from behind the others: the eldest daughters of the home.

One good look at Shay and at my own bedraggled state broke all barriers. Hospitality is inbred as sacred duty.

"Ah! Ah! *Bismillah!*" the toothless grandmother exclaimed as she threw her hands in the air. Headwife clucked maternally and ordered the girls to help carry Shay into the warm, sooty kitchen. "*Bismillah!*" she chanted as we picked her up.

Before entering a locked room, before eating, before undertaking almost any task, Muslim Berbers invoke Allah's blessing with the incantation, "*Bismillah!*—In the Name of God!"

All of us were strong from heavy work in house, fields, stables, gardens, orchards, and from striding mountain trails. The women and I soon had Shay deposited on a soft mat and stripped of her wet clothes. They had prepared a pallet close to the heat of the "stoves." One large clay pot of hot water rested on its side over the rock fire ring, and another warmed over a *kanun*, a three-legged charcoal burner.

Through intermingled bits of Arabic, French, and grunted sign language, I was encouraged to strip and wash, too. Bathing in the dead of winter is very unusual here, but this event had the flavor of a ritual cleansing. The two girls giggled quietly in nervous embarrassment. Community bathing is common, but watching a strange white woman wash by their kitchen fires was not.

The warmth of the water and heat of the kitchen couldn't hurt Shay, and I must admit the warm wash felt delicious on my own aching muscles and clammy skin. As I relaxed, I was overcome by the need to sleep. The last thing I remember was drowsily watching the two older women sprinkling salt on Shay's wet hair and tying a woven strand of wool threads around her wrist for good luck.

When I languidly opened my eyes, I spent several minutes staring at a hand talisman imprinted high on the rock across the room. Still groggy, I stayed curled in the fetal position, moving only my eyes downward until I saw kneeling female figures silently murmuring their worship.

As long as it was prayer time, I closed my eyes again to talk with my Heavenly Father. We had lots to talk about. I alternately dozed and prayed, but as I started in on my requests for Shay, my lassitude dissipated instantly. I hadn't seen her in the room.

I sat straight up to be struck blind, this time by sunlight glancing off the snow and in through an open door. The chill that, at the same time, hit an unexpected amount of skin, prompted me to discover that I'd collapsed naked last night. My hostesses had simply rolled me onto a rug against the wall and covered me with a scratchy Marmucha carpet. Blinking, I tried to rub my sunburned retinas back to normal.

My traveling clothes were nowhere in evidence—probably gone forever—but beside me lay a neatly folded, ankle-length ceremonial dress. The delicate robin's-egg blue silk was elaborately embroidered with metallic gold thread that sparkled in the sunbeam. Also gleaming in the pool of light were a silver coin headdress, wide silver belt, several bangle bracelets, and an amulet necklace. Underneath these treasures were two squares of heavy woolen cloth meant to be wrapped around my feet. As quietly as possible, I began to pull the shimmering garment over my head.

The three women raised up and sat back on their heels, each fingering loops of wooden *misbahas*, or prayer beads, sometimes known as "worry beads." They were counting off the ninety-nine beautiful names of Allah. I caught one or two, though their tongues were quick and my ears were slow. There was "the Exalted," . . . "the Generous," . . . "the Creator," and "the Compassionate." Long dormant brain cells seemed to be activating with a few days re-exposure to the sights and sounds of my previous life, I thought as I snapped the belt round my waist with a satisfying click. The little girl who loved to play dress-up lived on somewhere inside this rapidly aging body.

With my fingers, I unratted my tangled mess of hair the best I could and pulled the dangling headpiece low onto my forehead. It was snug, but an irresistibly glamorous way to keep the hair out of my eyes. Neither could I resist, at least temporarily, clasping on each wrist a thick silver bracelet inlaid with colored stones. The ceramic talisman necklace was another Hand of Fatima. Like the larger one on the kitchen wall, it was used to ward off the evil eye and bring

149

good luck. I left it on top of my rolled mat.

"*Sbah el-khir*!" Headwife said as she finished her devotions and introduced herself as "Zara." The two girls twittered as they rolled up their prayer rugs and stashed them in their corner.

I laughed, too. The lady had greeted me with a "Good Morning!", though from the angle of the sun, and their prayers, I knew it had to be past noon. These women had been up many hours already.

"*Sbah el-khir*!" I responded to Zara. I recognized her from last night. I'd been right. As she introduced herself, she proudly made it known that she held the position of first wife. Probably only in her late twenties herself, but already looking ten years older, Zara introduced the third wife, Tudda, still in her teens, and very pregnant. Tudda, and the sloe-eyed girl next introduced to me, were not the two preteens I saw last night. This was a very extended family indeed.

Fatna, who turned out to be Tudda's younger sister, was lovely both by art and nature. The pampered teen was dressed in formal orange silk and had slick black kohl lines around exotic eyes. Henna paste had been daubed on her face to redden the skin, and she was adorned with pounds of metal jewelry.

With an openness extremely unusual for these mountain people toward a foreign outsider, the two wives confused me thoroughly as together they gushed something about the *moussem* at Imilchil. Finally, I got the picture.

Fatna had left her far tinier *doaur*, or farming hamlet, in the High Atlas and was in this household being prepared for marriage at the autumn assembly. Zara and Tudda were making sure she would bring honor to the family by attracting a good match come fall.

This was an exceptionally wealthy household, and Fatna was more fortunate than many rural girls these days. With their large families too impoverished to provide for so many mouths, a great number of young girls, and boys, are, every year, forced to make their way to the *bidonvilles* encircling the large cities. Like Ali did, they struggle to survive and earn a living any way they can. With no education, their options are few and dismal. Yes, Fatna was very fortunate.

On my second trip to Morocco with the medical ship, a dispensary team and I attended one of the Ait Addidou tribal gatherings—along with a swarm of tourists. From what started as an annual clan reunion, pilgrimage, and festival, the Imilchil *moussem* has turned into quite a show.

Each September, on the plain between the waters of the two spellbound lovers, Tislit and Isli, doomed never to consummate their own love affair, dozens of couples from this tribe are promised or wed at a huge marriage mart.

Among gigantic chieftain's tents, and booths tended by shrewd businessmen certain to sell wedding presents, nervous young men and women of marriageable age wander through the holiday crowds dancing to the beat of tambourines.

Prospective grooms wear white *djellabas* and silver daggers. Fatna, and the other hopeful brides, will be concealed beneath lovely voluminous robes and as much jewelry as financially possible. But their faces will be uncovered, except for a bandeau of coins across the forehead—much like the one I was wearing now.

When a likely boy and girl discover each other in the midst of the crowd, they walk hand-in-hand among the revelers awhile. Then they return to each of their families, informing them that it's time to discuss the marriage contract. A public notary must register all agreements. For a marriage to be legal today it's no longer sufficient for the partners to recite just the *fatiha*, or first *surah* of the Koran. The multiple ceremonies are performed each evening.

This September *moussem* is the Ait Addidou's equivalent of dating. In the cities, a smitten man goes to a girl's family directly and asks to take her as a "free wife." They're often cousins, because it's hard, even today, for men and women to observe each other outside a family setting. However, with more and more women working, contracts made without the girl's consent are giving way to Westernized styles of courtship. Except in little Malika's case, I thought, remembering what had happened to Sami's younger sister.

Unfortunately, the old *Mudawana*—the "Law of Personal Status"—is very much in effect. This gives a husband the right to unilaterally dissolve his marriage by simply pronouncing the formula: "I repudiate you." So divorce is common. Most men don't make enough to support more than one wife and family at a time, even if the wives are also employed.

Not knowing the terms in her dialect, I congratulated the girl as best I could. "*Toutes mes félicitations*, Fatna. *Que Dieu vous bénisse*. I am sure you will marry well. *Ah . . . vous marierez bien*." The pleased girl's hennaed skin colored a deeper pink. As Zara embellished my French in Tamazight, Fatna covered her face with her hands and squealed happily behind them. Zara and Tudda hooted their customary ululations.

Berbers can be loud. They love to howl and dance and sing. At festivals they can dance all night, or they'll choose male and female teams to yell extemporaneous songs full of insults, humor and double-entendre at each other.

"*Merci, madame*." Fatna managed.

Amenities over, the practical Zara got back to business, just as I needed to do. It had been distracting to float away on their little bubble of happiness, but I couldn't shelter in this warm kitchen forever.

"*Zid*!" she commanded, before I could ask my question. As first wife, she outlined the day's tasks and gave orders about the couscous to the younger women.

Tudda and Fatna obediently scurried over to check the bubbling, savory mixture of grain as well as various bowls of vegetables on the far side of the room.

Zara would be as Fatna's *gallasha*, not only preparing the girl for marriage, but, also looking after the new bride's belongings and her well-being during the first weeks of life in her husband's home.

With her intelligence and forceful personality, it was evident that Zara received the respect of the lesser females. That's not always the case. The in-fighting among the sometimes numerous women in Maghreb households can make life miserable for everyone. I suspect that's why men reserve a "no-girls-allowed" for themselves.

There was no sign of the grandmother or the younger girls. Our clothing told me that this was a festival day of some kind. The others were undoubtedly assigned jobs elsewhere in this large home. Women in a household of this size carry out chores according to a rotation system requiring alternate periods of intensive work with periods of rest.

Who was with Shay?

As if reading my mind, Zara turned back to me and said, in French, "Your friend is in the women's bedroom above. I am taking her coffee and barley soup. We will take enough so you may eat with her there."

Noticing the look on my face, she explained, "My husband's business with outsiders has taught me many things. I must warn you, do not fight your fate. As the saying goes: 'Don't put anything into the pot that might stick.' If you obey, you will survive."

Like she was surviving?

I followed Zara to the fire ring, and helped her as she loaded a lacquered tray. When Tudda called Zara away to inspect a basketful of dried corn, I couldn't resist taking a peek out the open door.

In spite of the woman's advice, maybe I should make a run for it. Distract the guard, get away and bring back help. But who? And run where? They might punish Shay for my escape. Even if I *could* get help, the Volcares would be over the border by the time that help could get organized.

I inhaled the brisk, free air. The pull for self-preservation fought with my conviction to stay with Shay. There were Joe and my kids. I might never see them again. But how could I leave my friend now? God hadn't died in the night. He'd give us both a chance to get away. The time just wasn't right yet.

A familiar sound caused me to instinctively pull back from the doorway. Within seconds, there was a muffled *whump* as a clump of snow landed squarely in the opening and half-buried the surprised Volcare doing guard duty a few yards away.

I could hear childish laughter floating down from a few stories up. The deliberate avalanche had clogged only half the entry, so Zara could poke her head far enough out the gap near the top to scream various threats upward toward the flat roof.

We both saw the angry guerrilla stomp and spew his way out of the snow mound and take off up the hillside path outside the house.

"*Bismillah!*" Zara thrust the platter of coffee and soup into my hands, hiked up her skirts, and exited the kitchen at a dead run. Torn between fear and amusement themselves, both Tudda and Fatna scampered after her, not wanting to miss the excitement.

I wavered there. I could dig my way out and over the snow blocking the unguarded doorway. My feet were wrapped only in wool rags. My dress was beautiful, but not practical for winter hiking. All I could see beyond this hillside were higher steep peaks thick with frozen whiteness.

Mendoza had chosen an effective prison, and the correct prisoners. I went in search of Shay.

 20

Oddly enough, tonight the family was celebrating a version of Id n Usggwas or New Year's Eve. Though at home we had turned our calendars weeks ago, the Muslim year is figured differently. It's shorter by ten or eleven days, and months are designated according to the sighting of the moon's phases.

Changing years tonight could also just be a custom peculiar to the local clan. Berber tribes like to do things their own way. They choose which superstitions, dogmas or traditions they'll adopt. In this modern world, these barbarous heights are still the unconquerable *"bilad al siba"*—Arabic for "land of insolence and dissidence."

Its peoples' "insolent" love of independence, and their passionate dispositions, have, led whole groups of them to embrace schismatic Muslim sects that promote folk religions thinly disguised as Islam. Maybe the family belonged to one of those.

My sense of time was skewed, but I decided this had to be

Thursday. So not only did this evening's sundown bring on Friday, *El Jamaâ*, the regular Muslim holy day, but, for whatever reason, Zara said it also ushered in *Ras el Am*, New Year's Day. Even if this was only a local observance, the whole mountain community, and several surrounding communities, would certainly shut down for the occasion.

That might explain why Mendoza wasn't present as Shay and I sat with the family on the stone floor of the main room, scooping bites of the traditional "couscous-with-the-seven-vegetables" out of one common bowl.

Like these Berbers' New Year's bull that balances the earth upon one of its horns while its feet rest on four eggs, the Volcares leader faced an awkward problem. Arranging quick transport out of these mountains for a large group on a major holiday (and day of prayer) rivaled the imaginary animal's task.

As we ate, the Ancient One—the family patriarch—repeated the customary tale about New Year's Eve, when the mythical bull holding up the world flings the earth from one horn to the other. Unless the couscous-with-the-seven-vegetables is prepared, and the first bite of it fed to a calf, the world will slip during transfer and fall down into darkness.

It appeared that the calf had been correctly fed, and the earth had been safely repositioned, because this was a jolly assembly of aunts, uncles, children and cousins.

New Year's festivities are sweet, cozy celebrations that don't call for bloody communal rituals like the spring rite of *Aid el Kebir*, where sheep are slaughtered (with their heads turned toward Mecca) to commemorate Abraham's faithful willingness to sacrifice Isaac.

The New Year's holiday doesn't feature interminable dancing; or frenzied galloping *fantasias*; or the tense, day-long deprivations the month of Ramadan brings, deprivations accompanied by night-long carousing.

Up here, in the middle of winter, food supplies often run low. Yet these people readily shared what they had. Huddling close enough to touch shoulders, Shay and I sat among the women, ripping off small chunks of coarse bread and scooping them into the hearty grain mixture. The festive dinner also included corn, herbs, walnuts, and, as always, gallons of hot, sugary tea.

Shay had slept heavily until about an hour ago. Tonight her color was better and she managed to eat a little. She had a slight cough, but didn't seem to have much of a fever.

Thank God! In spite of our situation, I felt like celebrating. The Lord seemed to have brought Shay through her ordeals more or less intact. In fact, she looked much too pretty for someone dragged away by kidnappers last week and nearly drowned last night.

The Ait Addidou women had produced yet another fancy costume for Shay. Hers was chartreuse and spangled with silver. With the shimmering coin headdress against her short, red curls, which the awed girls had washed, combed and groomed with henna paste (to strengthen it and keep out parasites), Shay was an incongruous, but lovely vision. Several of the men present had a hard time paying attention to their meal, or to the patriarch's stories.

If our attendance here was for any other reason, I could have enjoyed the event as much as Kit and Lyssa love their dress-up tea parties. As it was, Shay nibbled nervously at her food with three fingers of her left hand, while clinging tenaciously to my left hand with her right. Zara's 'good luck' wool was still tightly wrapped around that wrist.

Her fingers dug painfully into my palm when a loud thud reverberated upstairs. It was followed by the sound of many, heavy-booted feet clomping in the front door and down the stairway.

Mendoza, his left arm caught up like brätwurst in a sling, tramped into the main room with an evil-smelling cheroot jutting out of his oily beard. The pretense of acting the righteous *ulama* was no longer necessary. Here, he could be himself. I could almost feel his relief at shedding that constricting role, like he'd peeled off a girdle worn all day.

At a jerk of his head, the terrorist leader, in clean army

157

fatigues and pillbox cap, stood aside for a parade of his bountifully-laden soldiers. Man after man entered the large room, scattering family members to the outside walls and stepping on dinner remains. Box after box was dumped on a pile where we had all been sitting moments before.

When the last man deposited both of his baskets, all the underlings went back upstairs, except for Mug and his tall partner. Those two unslung their weapons and leveled them at Shay and I.

My little friend, without flinching, looked over our captors' heads, and, with her mouth set in a stubborn line, lifted her chin an inch higher. Shay always did hate to be pushed around. Whatever you told her she couldn't do, made her go out and do it perfectly, just to prove you wrong.

She gave my hand a squeeze. I squeezed back and lifted my chin.

Meanwhile, Mendoza, the Ancient One, and a tough, older clansman—probably Zara's husband—finished their bargaining in Tamazight.

At the great-grandfather's nod, cousins, uncles, and sisters moved toward the heap of goods. Adults began to break open boxes. Soon they were reveling in the food, cloth, and medicines they found. The new treasures were handed around the family circle and cooed over. The children were dashing about, squealing in agitated delight.

Now I knew why they celebrated tonight. It may have been like New Year's to them, but the party was over for us. Our keepers had been paid.

"This way, ladies, if you please," said Mendoza with a sarcastic flourish.

His armed goons motioned us out of the main room and marched us up the small flight of steps to the front entrance.

Before we could be pushed outside into the frosty night, Zara rushed up the dark kitchen stairs. She carried our dried leather boots and two striped woolen *djebellas*. Chastising Mendoza boldly in rapid-fire Arabic, she handed the clothing to Shay and me.

My heart leapt up in fear for her. Hadn't she seen the madness in Mendoza's eyes? But his successful deal must have given him temporary equanimity. He regarded her with the same disdain one allows a buzzing, but harmless insect.

"All right, put those on here. But hurry," he ordered. Hostages with pneumonia wouldn't be desirable commodities.

I had yet to see him in a coat of any kind. The zeal burning within must have kept him warm enough.

Mug and his buddy, who was not only as slender and as pointed as a minaret, but who also bore an untrustworthy walleye that drifted back and forth under a drooping lid, bravely stood guard while Zara knelt down and helped us pull on our boots.

"Be careful," she hissed in a barely audible mixture of French and Tamazight. "It is the season for evil mischief by the *Jinn*. Watch out for *Buaû*—the witch with goat's feet who roams these mountains during darkness."

She slyly tried to press carved charms into our hands. "Take these against her spells."

Zara leaned far over Shay's stubborn buckles, shielding her words from the men. "The *shayatiyn*—the devils—that take you attract the evil eye. I think Allah has already given you much luck. These amulets will help you keep it. Then the angels will protect you."

"*Shoukran. Merci*, but no . . . *non*, Zara," I said, shaking my head slightly. Mendoza had already gone outside. The two men were growing bored with this duty and had begun to make hurry-up noises.

"No thank you, Zara," Shay echoed in a raspy whisper. She waved off the fetishes with a low palms-up motion.

"We are *Masihi*—Christians. We are God's children," I said. Shay could do this better with her grasp of Moroccan dialects, but she remained uncharacteristically quiet. She encouraged me to continue with her weary smile.

I forged on, explaining badly with my rusty vocabulary. "*Jinnis* or witches or luck have no power over us, Zara. Our

Father, God, has given us His Spirit to live inside us. Jesus is our strong, loving Savior. He will protect us from evil."

Zara's wide eyes were full of disbelief.

*Please, Father, bypass my faulty human words and speak directly to her spirit.*

The hard steel of yet another gun was poked, this time, into my chest. "Move. Now!" French seemed harsh and strange coming from Mug's mouth, which was half full of teeth as brown and broken as his face.

"*As-salaam alaikum*—Peace be upon you," Zara whispered as she was shoved out of the way.

"*Wa' alaikum us-salaam*—And upon you, peace," Shay blessed her too.

I nodded my agreement as Zara backed into the stairwell and disappeared.

The terrorists marched us out into the winter night. I remembered that Dick had given me several Christian tracts explaining the basics of our faith in both Arabic and French. They had been in my *choukhara*. I hoped whoever here ended up with my pouch could read. I prayed someone would read one to Zara.


"Oh, Eve, I wish like anything you hadn't come. But, of all people, I'm glad you're here. Does that make sense?" Shay squeaked, her voice hoarse from all the abuses of the last week.

I couldn't see her face. We were sitting on the frozen ground, handcuffed back-to-back.

My vision was also hampered by the *yashmak*, a double full-face veil that Mug and his buddy had so thoughtfully provided. It was claustrophobic, like wearing a pillowcase over my head.

I rotated my eyeball painfully until I could peek out of the tiny gap allowed, so women wearing them can remain mobile without killing themselves.

Out of my peephole I managed glimpses of Volcares loading the large helicopters poised on the floodlit plain near the Volcares' camp. I could see that this high, flat, private plain was why Mendoza came to Imilchil.

Government helicopters routinely make supply drops to snow-bound Berbers during winter months. If these choppers were Moroccan government issue, as their markings suggested, the scope of Mendoza's conspiracies was very large indeed.

"I know it's selfish of me to be happy to see you in the middle of this mess," Shay went on. "But, for *you* to appear out of nowhere to save me, it's . . . well an honest-to-goodness miracle!"

"We're sitting here all tied up in a pretty package, waiting to be shipped to our new Libyan owners. I don't call that 'saving' you."

"And now that there's two of us, the police or the army or our embassy . . . somebody . . . will get involved.

"God sent you as an encouragement to me. Maybe for you too."

"I'm not real encouraged at the moment."

"Oh, Eve," she sighed. "We've been so busy and far away these last few years. At least this way we can have a nice, long visit."

That's Shay, ever the optimist.

When I was able to get a word in edgewise, I explained the situation to her—who the Volcares were, why they'd abducted her, and how I'd gotten here. Shay'd been told nothing, just left to assumed she was the random victim of terrorists.

"Poor Malika!" was her first comment after hearing the story. "And Sami! . . . That he came with you! You can see what a tender heart he has."

Shay was alternately thrilled over Malika's interest in Christianity, and furious about her father's treatment of her.

That was classic Shay, too. If ever anyone lived above, or

161

in spite of, circumstances, it was my best friend. I never remember seeing her concerned about her own comfort, or safety.

There were times over the years I'd gone ahead and done the practical worrying for both of us. But, there were other times when her bountiful, buoyant faith kept the two of us afloat with a double measure of courage.

The high country began to resound with the whining heave of revving jet turbines. The uproar increased with the *chop-chop* of massive rotors whirling into action. There were staccato-shouted orders, and heavily shod feet stamping back and forth in haste.

Shay fell silent. I wanted her to rattle on, and defeat the violent noise with words of hope.

Maybe tonight her throat was too sore to compete with the clamor around us. Could she have fallen asleep? She'd slumped back against me with her head resting near my shoulder blade.

Then my overworked ears caught a scratchy snatch of a tune.

"Shay, are you singing?"

She straightened her spine a bit so I could hear better. "I was humming Psalm 121 to myself," she croaked loudly. "You know I have a rotten memory. But if I put the words to music, I can remember them."

"Sing it to me, Shay." I turned my head to the left and lay my ear against hers. Her head felt hot even through the veils.

"I always think of it whenever I'm in the mountains. The promises are really appropriate," she whispered.

The ear-splitting din kept trying to rip her song away from me, but I strained to hear every soothing word.

With her voice crackling, she sang to a simple, plain-song melody:

> I will lift up my eyes to the mountains;
> From whence shall my help come?

My help comes from the Lord,
Who made heaven and earth.

He will not allow your foot to slip;
He who keeps you will not slumber.

Behold, He who keeps Israel
Will neither slumber nor sleep.

The Lord is your keeper;
The Lord is your shade on your right hand.

The sun will not smite you by day,
Nor the moon by night.

The Lord will protect you from all evil;
He will keep your soul.

The Lord will guard your going out and your coming in
From this time forth and forever.

Her hymn faded away and she rasped another rattly cough. Between our backs, I twisted two of my fingers around a couple of hers.

"You're right," I said. "He knows where we are."

# 21

Once again, I was flying through the dawn.

It crept into the thick little portholes of the gigantic helicopter; then the new light spread until it brightened even the inside of the infernal *yashmak.*

If I survive this trip, I'll have a terminal case of bags and bloodshot eyes from lack of sleep. From now on, I may always want to wear a veil over my face.

Baggy eyes were the least of my worries. Shay, handcuffed to the bulkhead on the floor beside me, was sleeping; but there was a lot of phlegm in her fitful breathing.

Mendoza was in a foul mood, and his ill-temper affected his troop as well. With the sixth sense of the sightless, I felt their agitation ricocheting off the walls of the copter. The restless shifting and muttering of the men sounded like frightened cattle in a cargo hold.

I'd been told their clients were not sympathetic about a change in schedule. Mendoza held me personally responsible.

Before sunrise, he'd plucked off my *yashmak* with a jerk, and bent over me. He held my face up to his with a handful of hair. His breath stank of foul cigar, garlic, and madness. Uncharitably, I hoped I'd picked up head lice at Zara's, and that he'd catch a bad case of them. I know I should have been more appreciative. He *had* taken off the pillowcase.

"Y-y-you need some counseling, *a-a-asna estupida*." He tried to bellow, but his vocal chords were too short for a powerful bass, and the intensity of his anger caused him to stutter a little.

The maniac wasn't suddenly concerned about my mental well-being. "Counseling" is the euphemism for the beatings that, under Islamic law, a man is entitled to give to his wife . . . for her good . . . so she'll learn something and grow from the experience.

Evidently, the *Ulama* Mendoza interpreted that to include any handy female when the man in charge was put out.

He yanked my hair. Hard. "I have important friends I wished to do business with. They have a delightful little *ksour*, set in the middle of a charming oasis outside Taouz. From there it is such an easy plane ride over the border into Algeria."

The color rose in his dark face and his eyes bulged out farther than ever. "But now, due to your stupid interference, we had to delay the meeting with our most worthy Libyan customers, and re-route through a farther, and much less delightful spot." That was when he began to smack my jaw with the backside of his fat hand. Good thing *alems* abstain from jewelry, like rings.

"You had better bring a good price to be worth all this trouble, you . . . ."

Let's just say he called me more, rather uncomplimentary names having to do with my unladylike character. He had an amazingly good command of certain segments of English and Spanish vocabularies. Unfortunately, I understood the epithets in both languages.

When he stopped spewing filth and slapping me, he

mentioned, "If you don't excite the high-priced interest of our Libyan buyers, *Senora*, I will very much enjoy putting a bullet in your head." Then he punched me again, but in places that wouldn't mess up the face that was so shortly to be put up for sale.

Rico, Guy, and Sammy Schwartz, down the road at home, all received Bozo "bop" bags two Christmases ago. They'd punch those weighted blow-up clowns with all their strength, only to have them rebound upright, and often bop the surprised kids back on the nose. If I had my hands, it would have been easy to bop this clown back.

Then the lunatic hit me with the cruelest blow of all.

He quoted Scripture—correctly—at me.

"As a Christian, you should enjoy this treatment greatly, *Madame*. Does your Bible not say that 'whoever slaps you on the right cheek,'" he proceeded to demonstrate, "'turn to him your other also?'" Following words with action once more, he began to guffaw 'til he choked and his eyes were streaming.

His "counseling" over, his pique expressed, the little man threw the veil back over my face—crooked—and, chortling over his cleverness, stomped away unevenly, swaying with the turbulence of the chopper.

As I let go of the tears I refused to let my "counselor" see, my hands knotted into fists. Forget the "other cheek" stuff. I didn't have any left. Mendoza had hit both of them.

Anger had to be a healthier emotion now than cringing fear. *Right Lord?* As long as I didn't do anything stupid that would hurt Shay.

But I had to do something with this ball of white heat stuck somewhere under my heart. I was cuffed to the floor . . . .

Then it occurred to me—there are benefits afforded to veiled women that we Westerners don't appreciate. Behind the privacy of the covering, I aimed in the direction of Mendoza's weaving back. I stuck out my tongue and made the nastiest faces I could manage. The sound of rude raspberries were swallowed up in the constant roar from the jets and rotors.

It wasn't much of a bop, but I felt better.

The helicopter stopped bucking. Calmer air meant we'd passed over the mountains. To the east or south?

Mendoza wanted to go east toward Algeria—not west—but the morning light beating in through the glass above my head was shining directly on the left side of my veil.

With that clue, and the names "Zagora" and "Draâ" being muttered by men seated around me, I decided, we were headed south along the eastern side of the Atlas. Mendoza was following the pre-Saharan *ksour* route.

*Ksour* are fortified Saharan villages. When long ago nomads wanted to settle down to a farming life, they built a series of garrison-like houses (*kasbahs*) and villages (*ksour*) along the Saharan side of the mountains. The *ksour* route follows the last vestiges of water and plant life before they both give way to endless sand.

Sedentary farmers frequently needed to barricade themselves in, and survive behind high impenetrable walls to ward off sieges by marauding nomads. Saharan resources are meager at best, and desert dwellers often kill off the competition for food and water. Though fewer and fewer are left, today's *ksar* inhabitant still guards this crumbling adobe outpost—with a machine gun or a bazooka.

I remembered sitting with Aisha, old at twenty-eight, one warm evening on her brick patio inside the Tata *ksar*. In "market French" she explained, "Storks bring luck to a village. The storks have not come back to nest on our mosque tower for two years." She shook her head wearily, used up by her hard, primitive life. "What children don't die, will soon leave. Under the relentless desert sun, our *ksar* will die."

The sweet *kif* smoke was becoming thick inside the helicopter. It made me dizzy and drowsy. Lulled by the constant vibrations, and exhausted, I dozed lightly.

I was gliding high over groves of almond and olive trees clustered around *oueds* flowing out of the foothills until the desert drinks them dry. Soaring date palms—which "have their feet in the water and their heads in the fire"—were the last sentinels of life before the unlimited emptiness to the east.

It would be pleasant lying under the shade of a palm, near the oasis stream. I could hear the refreshing *oued* babbling next to my ear. But, there was no breeze. It was stifling, hot. So hot, my own head was on fire. I couldn't seem to catch my breath!

Panicky, I came to with the suffocating linen veil stuck to my nostrils. It was hot and humid in here from my own breathing. I writhed and twisted, forgetting that I had no hands; moaning because I couldn't claw the smothering thing from my face, and because the steel cuffs were slicing into my wrists.

Finally, by rubbing the side of my head against the metal bulkhead, I was able to peel the sticky cloth off. It dropped to the floor, and I inhaled quarts of stale cabin air already recycled through too many noses and tainted by too many "joints." My head was aching, but the fire was put out.

However, the stream bubbled on and the moaning hadn't stopped.

I opened my eyes to the horror of bloody foam flecking Shay's nose and blue mouth. She was moaning as she struggled to get oxygen around the fluid in her lungs. Shay was drowning.

"Mendoza!" I screamed. "Let me out of here. Shay can't breathe. We need a doctor." As the heads around me turned slowly, I added, *"Le docteur? El medico?"*

Some of the Volcares were staring with glassy eyes and mouths agape. A few, startled, had drawn their guns.

The great leader himself staggered toward me down the length of the aircraft. There was no turbulence now. Terrific! That's all we needed. A stoned crazy standing between Shay's life, or death.

*"Madre de Dios!* What else can go wrong?"

One more good reason to hate him. Mendoza, as a good Marxist, couldn't believe in any god. Why invoke His name in an oath?

Stay with the program, Eve.

"She needs penicillin, oxygen, and a hospital. Immediately." I inclined my head toward Shay. "She has pneumonia."

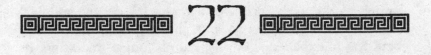

# 22

Headed west, the copter was flying low over the last hillocks of the Anti-Atlas, the end of the mountain chain bisecting Morocco north to south. Looking down, I saw thick stands of carob and argan trees. That confirmed our location, because argan only grows at the southern terminus of the Atlas range.

Despite the seriousness of the situation, I smiled as I recalled the sight of contented goats grazing on juicy argan leaves up in the branches of the trees. Those leaves must be very tasty. The goats ignore wicked thorns to climb up there for dinner.

And carob trees have, for centuries, been important to Arabic culture. Besides nourishment, their elongated black pods provide seeds that serve as jewelers' weights. Today, gold and precious stones worldwide are measured in carats. "Carat" is a derivation of the Arabic word for carob or "karab."

Jewels couldn't help Shay now unless they could buy our freedom from these madmen. I didn't have any in my pocket.

They'd already stolen my plain wedding band, my Timex, and my favorite little pearl earrings. And the Smith and Wesson.

I turned back to my friend and checked the oxygen mask over her face. Her lips were pinker, but I didn't like the erratic feel of her pulse.

The Lord was watching out for us. He was. This military helicopter had originally been outfitted for rescues, so oxygen, and a fairly complete medical kit were on board.

After being divorced by my parents, I did go to nursing school. Joe says I have a gift for working with the sick and hurting. Maybe it's because I know how it feels.

After working in third world countries on the medical ship, and being married to a "country doctor," I've had a good deal of experience in practical or "jungle" medicine. Its rules are: Use whatever's handy. Do what works. And its motto: Desperation is a great teacher.

Scrounging through the kit, I'd come up with a vial of sodium penicillin G, and a sterile syringe. After a little prayer, I tried to visualize the dosage charts from the Missionary Medical Manual I'd memorized so many years ago.

There was no one here but me to diagnose and treat what appeared to be the most virulent case of pneumonia I'd ever seen. Shay must have aspirated some horrible bacteria along with the lake water.

It had been quite a while since I'd done this. And then I'd always worked as part of team—a team of doctors. Was it like riding a bicycle? Why did a very sick Shay have to be my first solo patient in years?

*Help me, Lord!*

Then, as clearly as if a voice had spoken, I knew that 500 mg. would be the right dose.

*Thanks, Father. Now please guide my hands. Keep 'em steady. They seem to have developed an awkward tendency to shake.*

His assurance came again, deep within me. It's inexplicable, irrational, and supernatural. My hands stopped trembling. I knew I was working with the best team ever.

It was a smooth injection. The rude medication would cause an uncomfortable burning sensation at the inoculation site—but it could also save her life.

The entire contingent of Volcares seemed content to leave any treatment to me. I don't know if it was because nursing was women's work, or that I seemed to know what I was doing, or that they were all too zoned out on grass and hatred to care.

Their lack of compassion gave me back the use of my hands. After I saw to Shay, I used those hands to shred both *yashmaks* into strips. "For clean-up rags and bandages," I'd lied. *Sorry*.

Why not lie to these selfish, greedy, consuming . . . . My animosity kept me tearing and tearing at the linen until there was only a pile of stringy tatters in my lap.

The Volcares of this world will never care that I'd already spent most of my lifetime being held hostage, being treated as an inconvenient object, and being used as a pawn in someone else's game. That's why choice and freedom are so important to me. I'd rather be dead than a slave again.

Except there was Shay to consider. I'd have to work hard to keep my anger in check—for her sake.

In contrast, Mendoza, with his spleen vented and his Angst soothed by *kif*, acted like he didn't have a care in the world. Acceptable new schedules had been radioed ahead. He still had one healthy hostage to trade. Any good slave trader had to expect some losses during shipment.

With a shrug, he had the medical supplies brought to me like an indulgent father giving his toddler a toy doctor's bag. He really gave me the supplies because I wouldn't shut up until he did. In his benign mood, he evidently didn't feel the need to batter my marketable assets any more. As he put it: "You will—one or both of you—be the Libyans' problem soon enough."

Half an hour after I spotted the argan trees, Mug and Wally—for so I christened Mug's rangy companion with the roving eyeball—carried an unconscious Shay into a Blue Man's tent. This pair had apparently been assigned the task of herding us the rest of the way to market.

The drab sandiness around us; the faint sea tang in the westerly breeze (not at all like the dreaded *scirrocos* or *chergui* that roar in from the east during summer with their dry, choking clouds of Saharan dust); and this encampment of R'Guibat Touaregs, convinced me that we were somewhere in what used to be called Spanish Sahara.

If that was so, then we were smack in the middle of the Zone of Insecurity, the disputed territory Polisarios are fighting to regain.

Mendoza undoubtedly had rebel contacts here. With his background, they could be leftover Spanish colonists sympathetic to the cause—or to making money. Sympathizers here had to be willing to take chances, because this territory was well within the Moroccan-held and heavily defended perimeter of the berm.

An R'Guibat servant folded back the tent flap and led the men to a mat laid out for Shay. The girl wore one of the deep indigo blue robes that give this tribe its popular name. After she shooed the two Volcares back into the sunshine, she removed her violet-blue veil, revealing intricate blue chin and forehead tattoos—the very height of fashion for the women of the Blue Men.

The R'Guibats, too, are a proud and self-sufficient people. They can be very fierce. It's not unknown for them to raid unwary visitors wandering into their realm. These are Ali's people.

Blue Men rarely go into town. When they do it's only to trade their coveted almost-white camels, skins, or wool for blocks of rock-like sugar and bags of salt. Once at market, however, they'll stay all evening and join other members in dancing the turbulent and erotic *guedra*.

The tribe's men are tall, dark and angular. Often they wear

proud, pointed goatees. As they stride regally over the desert dunes, deep violet-blue robes float out over their *djellabas*. Their twisted blue turbans rub the indigo hue into their skin, their hair, and beards.

Their features have been dyed blue since the 1500s when an English cloth merchant visited a nearby port with indigo-tinted calico for trade. These people are not slaves to changing fashions!

The large tent, with its lavish rugs must belong to the wife of this clan's *sheik*. Her serving girl, with simple caftan, and none of the heavy amber jewelry higher class ladies display, was shy and ill-at-ease.

She backed into a corner humming a magic incantation under her breath. Sickness is believed to be the work of Satan's devils or of *jinns*, the invisible genies that reside in earth, trees, or animals.

I smiled to reassure her she had nothing to fear from us, but centuries of superstition, and yet another language barrier, couldn't be hurdled that easily.

The girl's low chant mingled with the murmur of male voices carried on the wind. "*Allahu akbar!*—God is Most Great!" they recited. Then: "Praise be to God, the Cherisher and Sustainer of the worlds; Most Gracious, Most Merciful, Master of the Day of Judgement. Thee do we worship and Thine aid we seek." It was the opening verse of the Koran.

I'd forgotten. Today was The Assembly: the Muslim sabbath and day of communal *salah* or worship. In absence of a mosque, men gather with their *imam* outside the camp, performing their required ablutions with clean sand, since there is no fountain or other running water.

Kneeling down, I checked Shay's temperature and fanned the ever-present flies away from her face. Even though the wind was chilly, the mid-day sun was making the tent too warm. Shay was sleeping more peacefully, and even breathing a little easier. I hated to disturb her rest, but the woolen robe she wore wasn't helping her fever any.

Once the girl realized what I was doing, she hopped over,

obeying her orders to assist me, and helped me pull off Shay's *djellaba* with a minimum of fuss. With a sigh, my ill friend settled back into a comfortable rest.

My *djellaba* was getting much too warm as well, and I'd suspected for hours that I wasn't the only resident. Fleas, lice, and who knows what else, were having a feast on my flesh. My hair felt crawly and there were itchy bites in every tender spot. I wished I could shake out the little creeps over a fire and watch the minute beasties roast and pop. I'd once seen an Algerian Touareg do that when he couldn't stand the massive irritation any longer.

How I craved an afternoon in a *hamam*, the communal Turkish bath where one progresses through different sauna-like rooms, each hotter and steamier than the last! I longed to scrub my skin clean, and pink, and free of vermin.

At the bathhouse, when you finally reach the hottest room, there are faucets of gloriously hot water, heated from outside the building by a large wood-burning stove. You are expected to spend hours soaping, shampooing, socializing, and eating oranges.

Better yet, I wished I was happily adrift in my old claw-foot tub at home. I wouldn't even mind being interrupted every five minutes by the never-ending procession of knocks; questions through, and notes under the door; or the kids' news bulletins about minor disasters.

The wave of homesickness and fear that washed through me threatened to undo the cocky nonchalance I'd chosen instead of the more honest, but dangerous anger.

I couldn't give in to fear. Shay and I were both still alive. God promised to never leave us or forsake us. There was still hope. All I had to do right now was get out of this infested robe.

Since Mug and Wally were watching, I knew I wouldn't be allowed to leave the tent, even to debug by a fire. I was stiff with the reminders of Mendoza's "counseling;" so it was difficult to pull the robe over my head. I emerged to find Wally standing so close his large, sharp nose was practically touching mine.

174

I screamed. That is, I started in on a good, loud one, perfectly high-pitched and screechy like Lyssa produces when she's really frustrated, but Wally clamped a long, gritty hand over my mouth. I tried to bite his palm and wrench away.

"*Non!*" he spat, looking over his shoulder.

The *khatib's* sermon was in progress at the meeting outside. He preached louder and louder to be heard over the whistle of the quickening wind and the snapping of tent walls.

Wally thwarted my shriek in time to avoid detection. The speaker's pious admonitions continued on undisturbed.

"I will not hurt you," Wally whispered in French when he was satisfied I hadn't alerted the camp. He didn't remove his grubby paw, however. "I need your help. *Comprenez-vous?* If you will not scream I shall remove my hand from your mouth." He looked at me expectantly. "Okay?" he added the universal word of agreement.

There wasn't much to gain by screaming—I had no illusions about anyone in this camp being willing to fight for my honor. And despite his shifty-looking eye, something about Wally showed sincerity—perhaps it was the way the sophisticated black uniform hung loosely around his bony frame.

So I nodded. Besides, I was curious.

He pulled his big hand away warily, not trusting me more than I did him.

"Be seated here." The enigmatic Volcare motioned at a mat opposite Shay. Once I was seated with his knees and elbows jutting out at impossible angles, Wally squatted nearby and launched into his story.

The servant girl, perched on a camel saddle in her front corner, kept a rigid, blank face that said she was working hard to hear every low word. But the slight furrow on her brow indicated she didn't speak French well enough to keep up.

I was struggling myself, not having had much call for French conversation at, say, the Kamas Falls P.T.A., or at Bible study.

"My brother's tent is in this camp. His new son has the stiff sickness. He will not eat and does this."

Wally, whose real name turned out to be Abd al Rahmen ben Nasir ibn Sebkha, stuck his bearded jaw out rigidly, and realistically mimicked horrifying spasms. We'd both seen those symptoms before. I could tell from the look in his one straight eye, that we also both knew most babies with neonatal tetanus die.

The man's pointed beard was no longer blue. Chances are, he'd left for the big city to seek a better life before he even had facial hair, but Wally's heart was here, and it was breaking. My enemy was human, too.

Thinking about enemies reminded me. The passage Mendoza threw in my face while he was slapping it, had stuck. It even brought along some others. They were the Lord's words of truth, no matter who quoted them at me. Tenaciously, they'd rattled around my mind all morning, convicting me about my attitude of self-righteousness, and about my response as a Christian to mistreatment.

Commands like: "Love your enemies, and pray for those who persecute you . . . ." (for Mendoza?) Or, worse yet: "If you forgive men their transgressions, your Heavenly Father will also forgive you. But if you do not forgive men, then your Father will not forgive *your* transgressions." I was in enough trouble here. I couldn't afford to cut off my lifeline to God, by indulging in rebellion and anger.

*Okay, Lord,* I finally prayed before the helicopter landed. *Give me that . . . that . . . love . . . for Mendoza and the Volcares You want me to have.* (My brain almost seized up over the word 'love.') I toyed quite awhile with variations of that ungracious little prayer—and another asking forgiveness for my own pride—between times of caring for Shay.

Now Wally was here with the Lord's pop quiz. My enemy was "hungry and thirsty." This was my chance to love my tormentor.

"I have seen that you know about medicines," Wally glanced at Shay. "Come and help *le bébé . . . Veuillez.*"

He'd said, 'please.'

I mentally cataloged the drugs in the first aid kit. Then I shook my head.

"The baby needs to be taken to a hospital, as soon as possible."

Even in the best of medical facilities, with round-the-clock intervention, fifty per cent of infants with symptoms that advanced die.

He misunderstood my declination. "In return, I will help you." He thought I was bargaining for a payoff.

"To get away?" I couldn't help asking.

"That, I cannot promise. Alone, you would have no chance in the desert, even if Mendoza, or the Polisarios didn't find you."

"Why would you help me in any way? What about your 'cause?' . . . What about Mendoza?"

Even as I spoke aloud, I weighed the risks of the R'Guibats' wrath if the baby died (which was likely), plus the cost of rekindling Mendoza's insane fury, if Wally was lying; against the chance that, somehow, this was our last opportunity to get away before being handed over to the Libyans.

Wally spat into the charcoal brazier, which spat back with a steamy *pop*. "Mendoza is a pig only out to make himself rich and powerful.

"Yes, I joined the Volcares for my beliefs, thinking here was righteousness, here was justice. Thinking they will help my people. But now I know the truth. I only put up with him to help my family walled outside, away from our home.

"Someday, I will slit Mendoza's fat throat." He fingered the curved dagger hanging at his side, but he kept it sheathed.

I was relieved. These people live by the Arab belief that once a man draws his dagger, he must draw blood.

"All I can do is try," I said, jumping up to recheck Shay, and grab the kit. Try, and then pray like crazy. I just had to trust Wally if he felt that way about Mendoza.

With all the tribe's men at prayer, and the other Volcares nowhere in sight, the tent encampment itself was deserted. Blowing sand whipped up by the wind gave a further illusion of safety.

177

I followed Wally closely, clutching the steel box with its red cross under my arm. The cold gusts blowing in off the ocean plastered the thin ceremonial dress to my body, and snapped the skirt smartly against my legs.

As the uncle wove in and out among the tents, I tried to keep my borrowed blue veil clamped on with my unoccupied hand. Once again a veil proved to be useful, this time for keeping a bit of sand out of the eyes, nose, and mouth.

Stooping into the gale, I watched where I stepped. Although the stiff breeze kept the hordes of flies inside the tents, hard-hearted scorpions were out enjoying the sun. My loaned *babouches* offered scant protection against their lethal stings.

We rounded a gay tent covered with goat skins and bright rugs. On its leeward side, Wally stumbled over a group of solemn children huddled on the ground. He must have stepped on one or two with his big feet. They made no noise as they scattered like frightened rabbits.

All of them vanished within seconds, except one frail boy, who despite his diminutive size, must have been about Ben's age. But, the hard, lined skin around his hollow eyes, and the hole where a nose and lip should have been gave him the face of an ancient, withered corpse.

With slow jerks, he raised that haggard face into the air as if to sniff for danger. Grabbing at the tent skins with jittery hands, he got his bearings. Then, through the wind and the sand, he wriggled himself away on his belly.

*Le bébé* was one very sick little guy.

We could only call him "the baby" because tribal elders refuse the newborn a name until it's certain that he will survive. How long had it had been before the elders allowed the blind boy with the severe cleft palate to be honored with an identity? Or would someone never capable of conquering the desert always remain in the mandated limbo between life and death? The child outside suffered as a result of birth defects. The tiny fellow before me was a textbook example of a vicious, and totally preventable disease.

He'd been born six days ago, a bit small, but healthy and beautiful. However, the knife used to sever the umbilical cord wasn't clean, and Chedlya, his young mother, of course had never been immunized against tetanus.

Right from birth *le bébé* had suckled vigorously. Since he was Chedlya's only child, she'd have enough milk. It's only when tribal women try to nurse a toddler, or two, plus an infant, that malnutrition is guaranteed for the children.

*Le bébé* ate heartily for three days. Then, day before yesterday, he turned away from the breast, refused to suck, and cried fretfully until he was exhausted.

Chedlya—who had already lost three baby sons—told Wally, and Wally, in French, described to me last night's massive muscle spasms. Every time she tried to soothe her tiny son by touching him, the convulsions grew worse.

Now the tortured, naked baby lay rigidly on his mat. Tied around each of his limbs were the woolen threads. His pad was hemmed in on all sides by every charm, amulet, or necromantic fetish Chedlya had been able to borrow or make. To ward off the evil eye, some were suspended from yarn, and hanging right down in his twisted face.

His puffy eyes were squinted closed in distress, and he was panting shallowly through a mouth already locked back in the grotesque parody of a smile.

*This little guy needs a bigger miracle worker than me, Lord,* I thought as I rummaged through my box. I prayed also that God's greater power would banish the treacherous spiritual enemy Chedlya had—in her ignorance and faith in magic—invited into this desperate situation.

The devil is real. These tribal people live their lives in fearful bondage to Satan. In vain, they try to stop his demonic attacks with the devices he provides to keep them in slavery.

Their Islamic faith is not enough to protect or release them, and they know it.

Only Jesus makes good on the promise that if you follow

Him "you shall know the truth, and the truth shall make you free." He also says, "If therefore the Son shall make you free, you shall be free indeed." Free from sin, and free from despair. Free from the devil's domination, and free from the power of death.

I know what Jesus promised happens. I know, because it happened to me. And Satan, Mendoza, the Volcares, the Libyans: they can't take my true freedom away from me—ever.

As politely as I could, I cleared away all the occult impediments confining the baby and asked Wally to take them outside, "for reasons of cleanliness." I certainly needed a clean spiritual scoreboard at the start of this fight!

Chedlya watched Wally depart, laden with the burdens. Her eyes were empty. She was resigned to another dead baby.

The Lord uses problems to teach us necessary spiritual lessons, and He certainly never wastes any other learning experiences. I gently cut the bands binding the baby's arms and legs, trying not to jostle him more than necessary. In that instant, yes, like riding the proverbial bicycle, a big chunk of my training in emergency procedures came back to me. I'd helped do this before.

I mixed vile-smelling, acidic paraldehyde—a nasty, dated remedy—with argan oil in a glass cup I cleaned as thoroughly as I could with boiling tea. I instructed Chedlya, through Wally, to swaddle the baby tightly in anything but wool, leaving an opening at the bottom. The mother remained frozen in a lump on the ground, as though turned to stone.

Wally, shouting in her own language, leapt into action. His years in the city had given him faith in doctors and in medicine.

Like a dog going after a buried bone, he tore into the small, carved trunks and duffle-like bags of belongings stashed neatly around the sides of the tent.

Seeing her tidy possessions flying through the air snapped Chedlya out of her torpor. Squawking at her brother-in-law (who stopped his chaotic burrowing), the lady went to a tooled brass chest and drew out three lengths of gossamer linen. With a surge of mother love, she tore into the fine material with her big yellow teeth, deftly making swaddling cloths out of the prized fabric.

Paraldehyde is corrosive enough to melt plastic. I only had one plastic syringe and some rubber tubing, so I had to administer the dosage by clumsy enema. Wrapping *le bébé*, and giving the drug, sent the poor little fellow into a new round of spasms. I prayed the medication's anti-seizure property would soon take effect.

I prepared a small amount of penicillin—I would have to boil and reuse the syringe and needle for Shay's next dose. Then I demonstrated to Chedlya, assisted by our male interpreter, how to express her breast milk. I tried to explain that I'd attempt to force feed her milk to her son with a stomach tube every three hours, so he could maintain enough energy to keep fighting.

And this plucky baby R'Guibat had fighting warrior blood flowing in his tiny veins. He opened his screwed-up eyes just long enough to glare at me for poking him. Good. If this sick little mite hadn't given up yet—well, then neither would I.

# 23

He was gone by midnight.

I'd finally convinced Wally and Chedlya that the intense course of treatment had to continue around the clock for, at the very least, a week (more likely, three) before there would be much improvement. *Bébé* should be in a hospital or clinic with trained personnel and sterile equipment.

Wally, who looked out for his brother's family while he was away on Polisario raids, commandeered a fawn-colored racing dromedary. Under a massive dome of stars that dwarfed and silenced even the immense desert, he hoisted Chedlya, and his tightly wrapped nephew, high into the camelback litter, mounted his brother's spirited white charger, cried "*N-sha Allah! Bismillah!*," added a "*Shoukran. Salaam!*" for me, and galloped off leading the woman and child into the night toward El Aaiún.

One of the camel boys shyly escorted me back through the camp. I didn't need a guide; I'd made the trip back and forth several times to look after Shay. But the company was nice, even if all I could do was straggle after him with what Joe calls, "bone-weariness." Any intern knows what it feels like.

This would make a great plot for one of those series Kit was addicted to. Something on the order of: *Sweety Adams: Junior Nurse on Safari.* I wished I could cuddle with her, and Lyssa, all our stuffed animal friends (and Ben & J.D., if they'd let me), and tell this as an exciting bedtime story.

At the very least, I'd get a merit badge for first aid. Last fall, J.D., my aspiring Eagle Scout, had practically mummified Ben in pursuit of a bandaging award. Maybe he could put my name in for an honorary one. But I doubt that they have Scouts in Libya. And if they do, they wouldn't award a merit badge to a girl.

There was still no sign of Volcares in camp.

When I'd queried him earlier in Chedlya's tent, Wally laughed. "Mumin, my ugly partner, is as stupid as he is ugly. To talk to you alone, I convinced Mumin that my people here are so grateful to any Volcare—for supporting our war against the invaders—I could easily find two to watch the prisoners, and give us a pleasant day off."

Wally blew a puff of contempt through thick brown lips. His walleye, normally pointed toward his ear, skipped over to take a quick peek at his beaked nose. "Mumin. Mendoza. All of them are lying, selfish swine."

I learned Mendoza was away completing transactions with the Sharawi. The other Volcares were unloading heavy rebel supplies at a wind-whipped site farther out in the desert. Mug must have seized the opportunity for a holiday like a faithful Muslim who's been offered the key to Paradise. Wally had provided him some entertainment and Mug was now somewhere snoring off its effects.

At last, my escort and I reached the tent. I couldn't wait to go in, look at Shay, then lay down. The servant girl was standing, waiting by the entrance. "*La bas!* All is well!" she was saying. Then she grabbed my arm as I stumbled and dropped the metal medic's box.

Protesting her hold on me—I had to see how Shay was doing—she repeated, "*La bas!*" and firmly sat me down outside, near the small, crackling fire made with camel-thorn. Squatting beside the flames and juggling two scorched teapots, was another, slightly older girl. The look in her eyes, and the sleeping infant bound to her chest told me her status had changed from servant to concubine.

These two were intent on showing proper hospitality to a friend of the tribe, and I was too tired to fight centuries-old etiquette.

While the older girl poured out a measure of "desert whiskey"—nomads' stronger, much sweeter-than-city tea— into the one shared glass; the first girl filled my hand with dates that had been dried and seasoned in sand. I hadn't eaten all day, so I popped them into my mouth, one after the other.

Finally, their social duties fulfilled, the girls took pity on me, and half-carried me into the tent to sink down beside my sleeping friend. I slept like the dead . . . for a few minutes.

The living God couldn't let me be. We had unfinished business. In those first moments of quiet rest, my defenses were down, and He called my name. Suddenly, I was fully awake. Admitting I was in over my head with the baby and Shay had softened and humbled me. And though they had come from Mendoza's lips, God's words had cut through the last of my excuses. I knew I must say what He had been waiting to hear me say for months.

I sucked in a deep breath, and sat up on my mat. Shay, still asleep, muttered restlessly beside me.

*"Okay. I leave it to You. Your will be done, Father," I whispered. "I give back to You: J.D. and Kit and Ben and Lyssa. And Joe. And Shay. The baby. The course of my own life. I release to you all our futures.*

*"Forgive me for taking all these things back into my own hands. For trying to put everything and everyone back under my control.*

*"Help me to serve You wherever You send me. Amen."*

I dropped off again after that, and when I opened my eyes the next time, it was as though I'd completely awakened from an overlong, restless sleep. I had the sensation of being wholly alive again, clear out to the tips of my fingers and toes.

The dirt, the bugs, the Volcares didn't matter. My body, my brain, my spirit felt effervescent; as light as the dancing sunbeams streaming in through the open tent flap. The burden was lifted from my shoulders. God was in charge, and I could trust my Creator to do what was right—for everybody.

I even prayed for Mendoza and Mug.


Mug, looking bleary and more worse-for-the-wear than usual, came in soon after I'd given Shay another dose of penicillin. She didn't look or sound good in spite of the antibiotic. And she hadn't regained consciousness at all this morning.

But her discomfort didn't concern Mug, or his new partner. As I packed the medical kit to leave, I wondered what they thought about Wally's disappearance. Volcares were probably used to desertions.

"*Yallah!*" At gunpoint, Mug—walking like the lines in his face had fallen inward till they cracked his skull—goaded me, sharper than necessary, back through the camp. The new helper, a sinewy young fellow with straight brown hair, was following behind, carrying Shay in his arms like a light load of wood. Myriads of shiny, curious eyes watched us go by in that first hour after sunrise.

Mug poked constantly at my sore ribs to hurry me past a lone Blue Man some distance from the group of tents. His once-blue robe was stiff and brownish-red with smears of fresh and drying blood. When he turned to look at us, I saw that his gruesome face had been half-eaten away by yaws. The wretched creature was preparing his breakfast near a large dung fire at the camp's perimeter. He was hacking chunks off a camel carcass with a gigantic scimitar. Dark clouds of greedy flies were keeping him, and the camel, company.

I fumbled with the case's clasp, thinking I could at least toss the man some salve—perhaps the tube of Bacitracin ointment. But, using his Uzi like a club, Mug angrily knocked my hand away. Then he propelled me forward by shoving his boot against my hindquarters.

Licking my split knuckles, I stumbled on past the doomed tribesman like he was a reverse Statue of Liberty. Cast out to the edge of open sand, he existed at the final boundary of human hope, and stood as a harbinger of the cruel, hungry desert ahead.

Shay and I were loaded onto the floor of a helicopter smaller than the one we'd come in yesterday. It was empty and echoing, so the Polisario deliveries had evidently been made. We were traveling light to the next appointment. Our arms were once again handcuffed behind our backs to the metal struts of a bulkhead, even though Shay was still unconscious, and her shoulders had to be contorted into an uncomfortable angle to do it. The brave soldiers must've been afraid that, sneaky as we are, we'd rush 'em, beat 'em up, and hijack their stolen chopper if they didn't protect themselves.

Mendoza and five of his men climbed aboard. The doors slid shut, and we were off—on what I knew would be the last leg of our journey. We were leaving Morocco.

"Where . . . ? Eve?"

Shay was awake. Over the engines, I could barely hear her. I leaned as far forward as my restrained arms would let me, so I'd be closer to her head, which was resting on the vibrating steel floor next to my left thigh. In the big rush this morning, no one had bothered with veils. Ignoring the complaint from my torso, I dipped my head even lower till her mouth was at my ear.

"Eve . . . " she rasped again. Her lips were dry and cracked, outlined with flecks of dried blood. "God sent you here to me . . . To see me through this . . . . Isn't He good . . . to let me see you one last time?"

"No! No, don't talk like that," I blurted out in alarm. "We'll have lots more time together. Why, just this morning, I turned everything over to Him. Everything'll be okay, now. He'll take care of us."

She coughed, and whispered slowly, "Oh, I know that. Everything will turn out right . . . Eve."

Tears stung my eyes.

Painfully, she continued, though her struggle to get enough air for speech was exhausting her. "You remember— no matter what . . . God is using this for good . . . ."

"I know: Romans 8:28."

"Yes-s-s-s." Shay's assent dissolved into a seizure of ineffective coughing.

"Here, use my sleeve." I pulled my bent elbow, covered with the limp fabric of the bedraggled blue dress, down as far as I could.

"I . . . I'm sorry . . . ." She was too weak to lift her head the last two inches it would take to wipe the sputum from her chin. I tried, but couldn't get my elbow any closer.

The terrorists ignored us while they slept or smoked. Mendoza must have been up in the cockpit.

"Don't try to talk any more. Rest now."

"I *must* say this," she flared with a vestige of her self. "When we are rescued, I want you to take me home to California. Talk to my Dad and . . . brothers about what happened here—and why. . . . Please say goodbye to Alex and Marguerite . . . Marion . . . and . . . others for me. Tell them that I love . . . . Will see them soon."

The words took incredible effort, but she was determined to finish. I didn't interrupt, but I had to clamp my jaws together to keep from it. I wanted to pour out soothing reassurances to cover the suffering—and make me feel better.

"Have everyone pray . . . Malika and Sami," she raised her eyebrows: Did I understand her distressed shorthand?

I nodded my encouragement, but I didn't mean it. I did not want to understand what she was saying, what she was doing.

"Pray . . . for their . . . father . . . mother . . . . Everything else . . . taken care . . . ." Shay's cheeks puffed out with each tussive blast. With her mouth closed she tried to contain the reflexive cough that kept shattering her message. "Except this . . . ."

She gathered her last fragments of strength.

"I have never had a better gift in . . . my life . . . than of having you for my friend. You . . . have helped and inspired . . . taught me . . . and kicked me in— she started a chuckle, but reeled it in before it could set off the reaction. "—the . . . uh, posterior . . . when I needed it."

A deprecative smile played over the chapped lips, and from her perpendicular position on the floor, her feverish, upside down eyes looked directly into mine. Shay had once had the foulest mouth I had ever heard; and I'd spent a lot of time in less-than-polite society.

"And you needed it . . . sometimes," I grinned back at her. Upside down, it might look more like a grimace.

But, she knew. Though we couldn't quite touch, an almost physical sense of warmth passed between us. She managed a nod, still smiling.

"Thank you for being my sister, my friend, all these years. I love you, and I always will."

She was spent. Her eyes slipped shut and her body sagged.

I was crying so hard, I wasn't sure I could answer out loud even if she could still hear me. "I . . . love you, too, Shay." I managed.

When the first blast exploded outside, and its following percussion jolted the aircraft, I was totally unprepared. My head lurched wildly along with the tossing helicopter, banging my cranium like a bell clapper against the steel wall before the pilot regained control.

Shay was deeply unconscious. Her head, too, lashed against the bulkhead. I attempted to slide my arms down the metal post behind me so I could swing my legs sideways between her prone figure and the inflexible panel. I was only partially successful.

Flames radiated out from a second missile. Its shrapnel ripped through the windows on the port side. The aircraft bucked and swayed in the second aftershock. The Volcares, several cut and bleeding, all scrambled to flee splintered glass and the blasting rush of wind coming in through jagged holes.

I'd thought with Polisario forces decimated, and the berm completed, that the Moroccan army had basically pulled out of the area. That would leave large portions of the sand barrier and the "Zone" unguarded.

Evidently, Mendoza had thought so, too. But his intelligence sources hadn't informed his navigator of the right spot. Not being knowledgeable about such things, I assumed those had been surface-to-air missiles coming at us. The Royal Armed Forces must be trying to blast us out of the sky.

That wouldn't necessarily be all bad. If we survived the crash—even if we didn't—we could be saved from being Libyan harem girls after all.

But there were no more missiles. Other than the louder roar from the engines, the whoosh of wind whipping through the cabin, and the moans of hurt men, all was as before.

Reckless, but clever, the egomaniac had run a calculated risk. The pilot must have flown over, and breached, the closest defense line at the weakest point.

The chopper swung eastward, into the sun once more. By the time Royal Air Force jets could be mustered to follow—if they bothered to chase one lone raider at all—we would be swallowed up by the vastness of the Sahara.

Mendoza was home free. We were on our way to Libya.

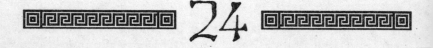

# 24

So, that's how I ended up here, with my arms and neck chained to the rock wall of a stinking cell in an abandoned Legion fort somewhere in the Algerian desert. I grated my cramped neck against the rusty shackle. Its harsh scrape brought me back to reality.

The stars had disappeared from my tiny portal. My review of the last two weeks had taken up the rest of this interminable night, but I could never have slept away these last hours of relative freedom. Rather than being a condemned woman awaiting the release of execution at dawn, I was waiting to be taken to a living death.

*"Quelle heure est-il?"*

*"... cinq heures et demie."*

Low male voices, husky from overnight disuse, grumbled outside in the early morning stillness. I heard the sentries stretch and scratch.

A pair of feet shuffled over to the voices. *"Il fait froid,"* whined someone not old enough to shave. *"Et ... J'ai faim."*

Course laughter. *"Toujours!"*

Then, the fellows warmed themselves with good-natured punches and scuffling.

In contrast, Shay was very quiet here in the murky dimness. At least Mug had let me cover her thin blanket with rotted straw from the floor. It had served as some extra insulation against the freezing Saharan night. For my comfort, he had provided a torn, stained tunic, that from its ancient condition, could easily have been a leftover from some long-but-not-dearly-departed Legionnaire.

We had to be in Algeria. Yesterday morning, after taking those hits, we flew, at most, another hour, certainly not long enough to get all the way to Libya. Besides, I'd caught the name "Tindouf" in a couple of Volcare conversations. That's an Algerian town of some size just over the Moroccan border.

The helicopter had landed near this ruin, which was the only distinct feature in an otherwise unbroken vista of endless rolling dunes and empty blue sky. Both land and sky spread until they met at the horizon as far as you could see in any direction.

I was marched across the sand at gunpoint, and in through the massive gateway in the uneven front wall. The thick, scabrous walls formed a large rectangle. Inside was a sandy courtyard with the tumbled remains of a well, and what was left of rickety, wooden barracks. Four stairways carved out of the high stone walls led to the flat catwalk on top. Up there, at intervals, there were embrasures built for the sand-blasted cannons now rusting at their posts. Today they made do for modern Volcare machine guns.

It was fitting that the Volcares made use of this rotted fortress. Mendoza's rogue army should feel as much at home in such a ravaged, forsaken haunt as did their Foreign Legion predecessors. It was clear that what ultimately motivated the Volcares of the present, like the Legionnaires of the past, were not political or religious ideals; but money, and twisted cravings for power and danger.

Under Mendoza's selective guidance, I knew now that the Volcares, following the Legion pattern, were also likely to be thieves on the run, mercenaries, or bullies itching for a fight. Some had to be criminally unbalanced madmen like their leader, who, for vaguely sensible political reasons, had banded this group of malcontents together, and turned out a cabal of highly trained, ruthless killers.

As I tried to wiggle my numb fingers shackled to the wall, I considered the former inhabitants of these crumbling walls. To this day, native populations hold no fondness for the Legion's memory. It is remembered as a gang of tough, brutal thugs who, in a colonial government's name, spent their time raiding desert villages. During those *razzias*, the soldiers gained a reputation for violent atrocities. Any romantic idealist that joined soon became hard-hearted when he realized the Legion was used wherever tribal uprisings were the most vicious. The French saw their ruffian forces as expendable killing machines that could be abandoned in outposts like this, to die of wounds, dysentery, or starvation.

I tried to shift my position on the dirty straw. Between the cold and inactivity, all sorts of extremities had gone numb. Maybe numb was what I wanted to be. The vibrant Zara had said as much. Me, who'd always fought to be so fully alive. How could I survive slavery?

Perhaps Tindouf had always been a way-station for the vast, cruel slave trade criss-crossing these sands for centuries. I'd been told that skulls, bones, and all types of mortal debris from humans and animals remain to mark the major routes where captives were marched through the desert. Children, or the ill who couldn't keep up, were left behind to starve where they fell. Defiant men were burned and whipped, or abandoned on the trail.

"*Salaam.*"

"*Bismallah.*"

More boots tramped about the courtyard now. A crow cawed and was answered by the shriek of a bird I didn't want to think about.

The soft *whishes* and *plops* must be prayer mats unfolding in the dust.

The slave traders of old had faithfully offered their *salahs* just like those religious Volcares out there were doing.

If Shay and I were fortunate, it wouldn't be long before our bones joined those others littering this heartless wasteland.

Boy, I was getting morbid! I pounded my legs against the ground in a sort of abbreviated flutter kick. I did toe circles. I needed to get some blood pumping back into my head. It was going numb on me, too.

The thought of my whole life being abbreviated like this —of not seeing or holding Joe, or my children again—was beyond bearing. Every time my mind wandered close to the image of a future like that, it skittered away, seeking refuge from the sorrow.

Over the course of the night, I had roller-coasted up through self-pity . . . anger at myself . . . anger at God . . . and back down to asking forgiveness and trying to regain the solid sense of peace I'd experienced in the Blue Men's tent only yesterday.

I had to face it. I was just plain terrified and I wanted out. I wanted the calvary to come rushing across the dunes to save me before the last minute. Why would God think I can take this?

The ancient door lock rattled and screeched. A stoic Volcare appeared balancing a slab of bread, some goat cheese, and a grimy pot of tea on a rough, weathered board. He lay breakfast down in the straw, then, with maddeningly slow precision he began to open each of my iron fetters. "Unghh," he grunted when finished. With a black fingernail, he pointed toward the food, already attracting eager flies, then at both Shay and I. Duty done, our keeper backed out of the door, then clattered his keys in the balky lock. He didn't stay to watch the resident rats race me for the bread and cheese.

I went to my friend first. "Shay. Wake up."

I couldn't rouse her. Shay looked extremely pale. She felt

clammy to my touch, and her breathing was rapid and weak. I had no idea of the state of Libyan medical care. I only hoped they'd give her whatever they had. Certainly a live hostage—especially a red-headed female—is more valuable than a dead one?

"*Balek! Balek!*"

Suddenly, shouted orders, oaths, and running feet exploded outside in the courtyard. Had our new Libyan masters arrived? Surely not. Panic was evident in the rush of Arabic.

The one airhole was too high up in the wall for me to see out. I went over to the bulky cell door with little hope, but I had to try.

The onslaught of the years had eaten away both wood and iron. As I jerked hard, I was rewarded with the protesting squeal of metal against wood. The antique hinges and bolts were coming loose from the decaying boards.

Outside, volleys of gunfire added to the uproar and hid any noise I made. Energized with purpose, I braced my foot against the stone wall, pulling and pushing at the first barrier to our freedom with both hands. With a cry of joy, I felt the nails holding the old lock wrench free.

Cautiously, I scraped the listing door open a few inches. The shadowy stone corridor was empty.

"Wait for me Shay. I'll be back for you." I slipped out of the cell, and, after pulling the door closed as best I could, ran along the bumpy hall in my stiff leather boots.

Blinking in the early daylight, I peered out into the empty courtyard. The Volcares were up on the walls shooting furiously at unknown invaders. A *razzia?* The fort was under siege!

Maybe I could get away in the confusion and bring back help to rescue Shay. I couldn't assume that the raiders on the other side of the walls would be more sympathetic to us than our present captors. For all I knew, the attackers were the Libyan clients who decided to forgo the 'cash' part of C.O.D.

There was a chunky coil of fairly new rope lying beside

the lopsided rubble in the center of the courtyard. A scant plan tumbled into my consciousness that, at the time, made perfect sense.

Every man I could see was up on the ramparts either shooting, shouting, reloading, or dying. Since their attention was elsewhere, I scurried out into the sunshine and scooped up the heavy rope. An old bucket attached to its end had been facetiously tossed into the useless well. I managed to hoist the unwieldy load up, loop it over my shoulder, and drag it all under the disintegrating remains of a slatted roof along the opposite wall.

Down this side, at the far end, was the stairway leading up to the rear wall catwalk. Poking my head out from my dubious shelter, I couldn't see any live Volcares up there to deal with. The only terrorist near the back of the fort was lying sprawled upside down at the top of the stairs. He was staring into the brightening Saharan sky with the unblinking eyes of the dead. All other guerrillas still moving seemed to be concentrating on defending the front gates.

I hefted the bristly hemp against my tattered silk dress, and shuffled toward the stairway. Broken gold threads dangled everywhere, and they flickered with reflected light. I hoped the tiny glints didn't signal my presence. Give me good old jeans for this kind of work any day.

I paused over the soldier's body to close his eyes, then gingerly stepped over him. But I wasn't strong enough to lift the whole mass of rope high enough. The dragging loops of the coil smacked his slack cheek. I winced.

"Sorry," I said automatically. When I realized he was beyond caring, the nausea kneading my stomach began to churn upward. With my back to him, I squatted down on the catwalk and took a few deep breaths. It smelled of smoke, dust, and . . . gunpowder.

Looking around, I saw the slain man's well-oiled machine gun lying on the rampart near my feet. I'd never used one before, but I knew I could if I had to. I made sure the safety was on, slung it over my head and secured the strap across my chest.

195

Fighting my long dress, I hunched into a crouch and crab-walked to the nearest corner where I searched for a place to anchor the rope.

My grand plan was to shinny down my rope over the back wall, get out of sight behind the western dunes, then run like crazy in a northwesterly direction. That way, I eventually had to hit Tindouf, or at least the Moroccan border, and, hopefully, some friendly natives. For it to actually work would be on the order of a miracle. But, he'd gotten me this far, hadn't He?

I was so absorbed in my hunt for a stable chunk of masonry on which to attach my escape rope, I forgot to stay down low as I moved around the corner and onto the side wall.

So, a moment later, when I glanced up, I could see out over the parapet. What I saw almost caused me to stand straight up in surprise.

I *did* drop the bucket on my foot, but gathered enough wits to limp back up into the corner turret for protection. There I allowed myself a wide-eyed, open-mouth stare out through the empty gun emplacement.

Blocking out the rising sun was a sandstorm swirled up by the pounding hooves of powerful Arabian horses and fast camels. Astride this army of thundering steeds were fierce, white-robed Touareg warriors. Whooping shrill war cries, rank-upon-rank they charged the fort with rifles blazing. It was so much a scene out of a classic movie, it was hard to believe they were real.

Then a very real bullet pinged into the turret and showered shards of mud brick on my head.

I huddled lower trying to decide what to do next, when a stray Volcare decided this would be an excellent time to retreat. The furtive way he looked around as he backed down the south catwalk toward me, told me he probably had thoughts of deserting over the rear wall himself. But I heard hooves pounding the sand close below me. Both our back-door plans needed revision.

The turret was merely an open cove affording no real hiding place. First, I had to get out of there. The guerrilla was still slinking backward. I might just make it around the corner before he discovered me.

Agonizing over whether to abandon my rope, I slid out of the small tower, only to find myself face-to-face with the defector. Doggone it! Wouldn't you know, the coward had turned tail and run the rest of the way.

I don't know who was more surprised. But I do know I recovered first—by a second.

Unconsciously, I had clung to my hard-won rope. I heaved it back and around more by instinct than intent, and the bucket caught him squarely in the nose. I'll never complain about bucking hay bales again.

Now I wasn't exactly caught between the devil and the deep blue sea, but the concept was appropriate. Dropping the rope, I fled around the groaning man, back down the stone stairs, over the body, and sheltered once again under the shadow of the slatted roof to think.

I knew what fate Mendoza had planned for Shay and me. I also had to take into consideration the soon-to-be angry deserter up there with the very sore nose. Not only had I witnessed his disloyalty, but his culture is big on revenge.

I figured I had better odds with the raiders. At least they weren't mad at me yet. Who knows, I might charm them into letting us go. Or, better yet, in the confusion, I might still get away over a sand dune.

The humiliated Volcare was on his feet. Realizing that going A.W.O.L. over the back wasn't going to work, he also had begun to weave his way down the staircase. His attention, so far, was mostly on his bloody nose.

Hating to turn my back to him, I sidled the rest of the way down the southern wall, then across the front toward the main gate. The roar of men and firearms was deafening. Raw fear hung like billowing dust in the hot, heavy air.

I pulled the potent, compact machine gun over my head, lifted the safety, and aimed, trying not to close my eyes as I pressed the quick trigger.

Wood splintered and metallic sparks flew as the hail of bullets I loosed tore at the three enormous locks on the front gates. As I got used to the recoil, I shot at the latches steadily until the ammunition gave out.

In the relative silence that followed, I heard the laugh. The Volcare with the swelling nose had me in his sights. Around the large bruised beak, his eyes and mouth were smiling the superior smile of a hunter who has his quarry cornered and frantic. He was enjoying moving slowly in on me. I turned back to the gate and tore desperately at the last bulky hasp.

But, with the din of battle, and his concentration on private retaliation, he didn't hear what I could feel. Someone was ramming the gates from the outside.

Anticipating the rhythm of my unseen partners, I impatiently waited, tensely holding my breath, and saved my energy for one last, best tug.

I could sense the next thrust coming, just as I could sense the gun inches away from the back of my skull. It was coming awfully fast—then the hardware gave way with a resistant scream—and, with me clinging to the crossbars like contact paper, the gate and I were flung out and around, slamming backward into the front wall with a huge shudder.

Probably nothing important was broken, but as I oozed down the wall like melting ice cream, I really did see stars and other UFO's whirling in front of my eyes.

"Eve. . . . Eve, are you here?"

I must have had stars in my ears as well. I shook my head to clear it and crawled cautiously to the edge of the gate.

My stalker with the bloody nose was semiconscious—another victim of the gate. But he was also firmly in the hands of a Royal Armed Force *Capitane*.

As I clambered to my feet, though the courtyard was now filled with men, horses, and machines, my attention was drawn to one tall Bedouin. Mounted on a regal black stallion, he was searching every barrack window, and he

198

seemed to be calling my name.

"Eve!" he shouted again over the uproar. Then he turned his head. Under the twisted ivory turban blazed a pair of white-hot turquoise eyes.

# 25

I stood riveted beside the gate, willing him to see me. Around and between us swirled choking clouds of dust, gnats, bellowing, smelly camels, and sweaty jubilant men. But the moment those angry, searching eyes met mine across the courtyard, the ice in them melted, and the heat in them turned up a degree or two more.

"Eve! Thank God!" I saw him sigh.

Joe spurred his Arabian crossways through the milling throng. Not bothering to rein in the horse, he jumped to the ground and gathered me into the circle of his strong arms. Shaking, I clung to him, drawing strength from his touch. I had found an oasis in this hard world, and he had found me.

Even with the grit, Joe's lips had never tasted as sweet as when he kept them pressed tightly on mine there behind the shattered gate. Then he ran those lips tenderly through my filthy hair, and my parched heart revived as he whispered all the words of love and fear and longing we had both felt this last week.

"Where on earth did you come from? Oh, I don't care!" I murmured in his ear. "Have I told you how very much I love you? Joe drew me to himself even tighter. "Eve, I was willing to do anything to get you back."

I pushed off from his chest and eyed his picturesque costume from Touareg turban to white robed hem to . . . his own comfy cowboy boots.

"I can see that."

"Can't ride proper without my boots, ma'am."

"Well, all together, you look heroic and incredibly handsome."

"You've never looked better, yourself," he whispered.

We didn't talk anymore for a while, until Joe reluctantly pulled away. Someone behind my husband was tapping his shoulder like he was knocking at a door.

Joe, with one arm permanently attached to my waist, turned sideways, and there, grinning widely, were Ali (who looked attractively audacious with purpling bruises on his cheeks and a rakish white head bandage), and Abu Talib, who, too, displayed a smile so luminous, it radiated light like a beacon in his polished black face. Soon all the back-slapping (with Joe), and hand-kissing (with me), attracted two more familiar faces to the reunion.

Leaving the tight knot of men surrounding Mendoza, and walking over to join our celebration were long-lost *Capitane* Bennani of the Judiciary Police, and the ever-cocky Lieutenant al-Aziz of the *Sûreté Nationale*.

"What happened to you in Marrakesh, *Capitane*?" I managed to blurt out the question I'd meant to ask days ago. My swollen larynx was causing my voice to check in and out like a boy soprano who's just hit puberty.

Crimson washed over Bennani's thick neck where it bulged above his collar. It crept upward until his whole dark face was a curious plum color. But the Captain was embarassed, not angry.

Ali cleared his throat and looked down at his boots in mock remorse, but not before he threw a slight wink my way.

"Your friend, Bakkali, may have a great future with our agency or the *Sûreté*, Madam Daniels," Bennani began. The Bakkali charm had claimed another victim.

"Or the diplomatic corps," smiled Aziz.

"Certainly, he has talents useful to many such organizations," Bennani nodded. "Since all has been forgiven, it now makes a good story—although it brings me no esteem."

"From the plane, I went to my close colleague in Marrakesh, hoping to obtain his services and some of his men for the mountain expedition."

Ali was having a hard time looking repentant. The corners of his mouth wouldn't stay turned down properly.

Bennani pinned Ali's eyes with his own. "Your friend," he said to me without removing his penetrating gaze from the younger man, "gave me the wrong information about the time and place of meeting."

"Oh, Ali," I exclaimed in a wail that slid up and down the scales, "you left them on purpose? We could have had more help?"

Suddenly, I remembered who we had come to help.

"Joe!" I grabbed at his billowing sleeve, but the squeak coming from my sore, dry throat was no match for the bluster and racket.

Ali continued shouting above the din, "I only wished to cut out what you call 'the red tape'."

"It worked out well enough," Aziz added, "since my distinguished cousin was already as far south as Marrakesh when it became known where the Volcares had taken you. And, as you see, it has all ended well."

"Ali!" I tried. "Joe—" I pulled again at his sleeve. "We have to—" My husband, caught up in the thrill of victory and unaware of my growing distress, accidently cut off the rest of my sentence with a loving squeeze. He had me so tight, I couldn't wriggle close enough to his ear to catch his attention.

The tough captain beamed at Ali like a proud daddy at a precocious son, and started in on a new round of accolades.

"It was he who gathered together all the information about the Volcare's—"

Abruptly breaking into this orgy of self-congratulation, a frantic Dick Foster appeared and muscled his way into the party. He hadn't lost sight of the original goal.

"Where *is* Shay?" Dick interrupted, wasting no time on niceties. "I can't find her anywhere in this mob!"

"That's what I've been trying to tell you all," I croaked. "Come on!"

I tugged at Joe's hand, and, though moments before, I'd felt like I'd never want to move my leaden feet again, I managed to dodge through the courtyard's swarm of soldiers, and their few live prisoners, at a dead run.

Joe stayed right with me, so as we ran I could shout, "Shay's really ill. She contracted pneumonia after she aspirated lake water."

"Near drowning?" Joe yelled back in disbelief as he loped along beside me. "How . . . could?"

"Never mind that now. It's worse than any pneumonia I've ever seen . . . not that I'm so experienced. I'm so glad you're here . . . for more reasons than one!"

Joe detoured to hail a medic and his supplies. Then they along with Dick, Ali, and Bennani, caught up with me, and close on my heels, followed me into the dark cell block carved out of the fort's thick western wall. The old door creaked shrilly on its wobbly hinge.

Shay must have already sensed that we were rescued, for she seemed to have a slight smile on her face. In the scant, murky light, only her face, pale and still, shone out of the shadows to meet my sun-dazzled eyes. She lay just as I had left her, with her body still half-buried under the straw coverlet.

Joe pushed past me to his patient. I rushed over to her, too. She looked like a fragile wax doll waiting quietly in her box for Christmas morning.

Then I knelt down and touched her cheek, and I knew she hadn't waited.

Joe slowly pulled his hand away from her neck, and

raised his cloudy blue eyes. "I'm so sorry, honey."

Shay had gone on home ahead of me. And she was far more free now than all the armies in this world could ever make me.

# 26

The rocky, lurching motion up here in the saddle brought back memories of clinging to the crow's nest on a choppy day at sea. Traveling with Joe, across Saharan sands by moonlight aboard this 'ship of the desert,' would have been unbelievably wonderful under different circumstances. As it was, only the desert's enormous void suited my mood. I closed my eyes and sank back against my husband.

To any curious observers, we were merely a large Touareg caravan traveling by night to arrive early at market.

Excruciatingly handsome, and swaggering around in the robes of a *pasha*, Aziz informed me earlier that once we crossed the Algerian border, the King's own Royal Boeing 727, waiting at the nearest berm station, would fly us to Rabat. "There," he'd said, "we will attend our necessary debriefings and diplomatic receptions." My friends were now going to be celebrated, perhaps even international, heroes. Aziz could hardly wait to play the part.

However, the formal celebrations had to wait until we were back in Morocco; since the agents, their assigned Moroccan army units—all of us—were officially uninvited, and essentially undercover, here in diplomatically closed Algeria.

Unfazed by that minor inconvenience, Bennani, Aziz, and Ali were already lighting up the night with their glow of good cheer. Periodically, they broke into ribald song, and laughter floated back to us from the front of the company. It had been a grand, successful adventure for them. They caught the bad guys.

The three surviving Volcares, handcuffed and discreetly tied to their horses, were being brought back in the caravan as well. Dick, just ahead of us on a racing camel, was helping the Royal soldiers keep an eye on them and Mendoza. It made him feel useful, he said, after the fiasco in the mountains where they "got chased away with their tail between their legs." Frustrated and grieving, Dick was heavily silent as he hunched over his mount.

Mendoza, had sworn, and threatened, and raved about wanting to be deported to Spain until Bennani had him gagged. Then an imaginative, or vindictive, sergeant threw a cloth over Mendoza's head, veiling his face. That sergeant managed to find enough cloth to veil all the others. They made perfect disguises in the moonlight.

I knew how Mendoza felt. I'd ranted myself while I was a prisoner. Even if most of it was inside my own head.

Mendoza was facing either the death penalty, or a very long time in jail. Moroccan prisons are not pleasant. Maybe his madness would numb the pain. Maybe he would search the Scriptures and apply the truth to himself this time. I knew who'd show up on visiting days, bringing the Christian gospel for him to consider.

Mug was among the mute bundles strapped across donkeys at the end of our procession. I had to keep telling myself that Shay wasn't back there being bumped around awkwardly—just the earthly shell she'd lived in. Abu Talib rode rear point, honoring our loss by watching over the desert and the dead.

After the morning's rescue, the men spent the rest of the day preparing the caravan, questioning the prisoners, and filling me in on what happened to them since the disastrous night we first found Shay. I spent most of the day cuddled up to Joe, either weeping at, or listening to, their amazing tales, until it began to make sense.

Turns out, Abu Talib has been one of Ali's most trusted friends since their childhood days in Goulimine. They had made opportunities to work together over the years.

Ali was warned beforehand not to trust Kef Rala, so he asked the stately, reserved nomad to be his eyes and ears. Abu Talib had hooked up with the traitorous Touareg just hours before we'd met them in Marrakesh. Though a man of few words, the dignified Talib sold the betrayer on his superior services as a mountain guide.

After killing Kef Rala and rescuing the injured Ali—while the Volcares were busy with Shay, and me, at the lake—Abu Talib was the one who rounded up Dick, and the four men of ours that he could find, and led them all safely back down to Khenifra.

On the way down that market track, they met a relieved Sami, who had stayed long enough to see me hauled out of the icy Tislit by Mendoza's men. All the way down the dark trail alone, he had worried over how to carry out my last requests.

Ali, in spite of several broken ribs and nasty gashes from the studded gloves, did what he did best. He took over. Angry at being bested, he flew into a fury of activity. First he hustled the other men and Sami back to Barbarossa's headquarters in Fez.

From there he contacted: not only Joe, who caught the next flight out, but the American embassy, the U.S. State Department in Washington, D.C. as well as every ministry he could think of in Morocco, until he convinced the Moroccan Director General (via the king, himself) to help us.

Knowing the "tentmaking" missionaries didn't want to jeopardize their work in Morocco by having their dual identities exposed; Ali shrewdly concentrated on *my* being taken hostage.

He'd laid it on thick. "Why," he'd told every official and newsman that would listen, "the kidnapping of this virtuous woman—"

"Hah!" I hooted.

"—in order to trade her to the Libyans like a slave, is a threat to family, motherhood, and the freedom of the American way. One doesn't even have to mention the balance of power, or international security, or diplomatic relations between two friendly nations."

"Your story made papers and T.V. all over the world." Bennani boasted on Ali's behalf.

That upset me until Joe assured me our kids had been so busy at Gina's, that they never had time to watch television. Neither did Gina or Nathan let on to nosy reporters that four of their brood of ten were actually ours. Bless them.

"After all that television time," Ali smiled broadly, "the King, a good friend of your United States government, decided it was prudent to seek the quick arrest of the seditious criminals.

Bennani was right. Ali could do *very* well in politics or in sales, or both. He would do well at anything he tried.

If only I could persuade him to try Christ!

But he possesses a headstrong, capable nature that has difficulty seeing any need for God's intervention. Within the human Ali, resides that rare blend of serpent's cunning, and dove's innocence. He is exasperating, but at the same time you have to love him.

Joe confirmed that another of Ali's men had successfully bought back Malika, Sami's sister, from her older relative. Both brother and sister were safe in Barbarossa's *dar*, and happily awaiting our arrival.

I forgave Ali for the slights to my gender and to my ego. He saved the translation work in Fez. He saved my life and others'. I would continue to pray for his eternal salvation.

For it was Ali, who realized that Mendoza's contacts would know the Volcares' whereabouts. He sent Abu Talib to Western Sahara to make inquiries among his fellow tribesmen.

When Wally—I could never think of the ex-Volcare as Abd al Rahim, etc.—got Chedlya and *le Bébé* settled in the clinic at El Aaiún, he let it be known he had information to sell.

Thus, through the grapevine, Abu Talib found Wally. Wally didn't even charge for the intelligence report.

"—to repay for the care of Karim," Abu Talib had broken into Ali's narrative to quote Wally's own words.

The novel sound of his melodious bass so stunned the other story-tellers that Abu Talib took over. In his succinct, quiet way, he told me that, due to the quick medical intervention, and the baby's own strong will (and surely prayer!); the little guy was expected to make it.

Wally had immediately named the baby Karim Something Something, after his father, who was still away on patrol with the Polisarios.

Armed with solid facts, and spurred on by Ali's efforts with both governments, the Royal Moroccan forces captured the Volcares' rear guard, left outside the R'Guibat camp. They also took back custody of their helicopters, which had been stolen during the flight from the factory in France to Moroccan air bases two years ago.

Bennani and Aziz got permission from their respective directors, and from King Hassan II, to make this covert foray into Algeria. It was understood, if they failed, such permission would be vehemently denied.

But they had not failed. Up ahead, strung like a necklace across the clear Saharan night, were the glittering lights along the wall of sand.

# Epilogue

The golden sunshine melted right through to my bones. It soothed the physical aches with its renewing warmth. I set Ted Bear down gently, braced my arms behind me on the marble bench, and turned my face up toward all those glorious UV rays. I stretched out my long legs inch-by-inch over the glossy patio tiles like a pampered cat after a lengthy nap.

Ali was in Rabat with Bennani and Aziz, still 'debriefing,' and working on his official future. We'd said goodbye to him and Abu Talib at the Rabat airport just before Ali—with Bennai's blessings—smuggled us aboard a BarBair plane for the short hop to Fez. That allowed Joe and I to escape the probes of press and governments.

The black man, after a solemn bow, and a flash of that wide, white smile, had dissolved into the runway shadows. He must already be back riding with the wind over the desert dunes looking for a frail blind boy among the Blue Men's tents. With his spare eloquence, I prayed he might convince the boy's parents to take a trip up north with him to see a place known as the Horm School and Clinic.

Now that the danger had passed, Dick came back from Rabat to rescue Treva and the girls from Barbarossa's hospitality, and they went home.

Joe and I returned here to the Dawson-Rhyses' house, along with Marguerite, Marion, and Robin Moffat. Even Sami Oukfir and sister Malika were staying at Alex's until they decided what they could do with their short-circuited lives. Zubaida, Marion and Shay's roommate, chose to stay at her family home north of Fez, indefinitely. Marguerite said happily that there was some hint of an impending betrothal to a "kind village widower," but that rumor was, as yet, unconfirmed.

Alex and Sami had started a series of ongoing debates about the Muslim and Christian faiths—much to the delight of both, I suspect. Shy little Malika was subdued and blue, but not entirely unhappy as long as she could be with Sami, whom she adored.

Last night, all of us here in Fez gathered to hold a memorial celebration for Shay. We cried together over our loss of her presence, and laughed together because of our assurance of heaven.

Tomorrow, Joe and I were taking Shay's body back to her Dad and brothers in California. I'd tell them about her last few days and cry with them as well. Marion was flying back with us—on a sabbatical—she said. But her nerve was shattered. I suspected she'd never return to Morocco.

I scooped up Kit's bear once more. I'd been cradling Ted on and off all morning as a down payment on the joy of gathering my children close to me again in just a few more days. I laughed and watched the sunbeams sparkle in the foam bubbled up by the fountain's dancing waters. Joe had carried messages from each of them, telling how much they had missed me. But I was thrilled the most by Ben's. I read it once more:

dere Mom

I relly miz you and i relly Like my name now. Angy tole me Ben waz strong and i think zo to.

P.z. cum home zoon

Love 4 ever
Ben Danielz

Joe came outside quietly. He watched the fountain, and me, for a moment. Then, crossing the patio in a few steps, he walked around my bench and sat on the brick border behind me.

Before my serene mind could scramble up any smart remark, Joe reached out and began to massage my shoulders. It was exquisite: slow and healing and kind. He had loving hands.

"Feel good?" he asked.

"Mmmm . . . hhmmm . . ." I purred.

Though there was a little sidecar of guilt attached to the idea, it *was* good to be alive. It was great to be me.

I'd found Shay, only to lose her, at least in this time and space. But God had taught me that finding and losing are all bound up together.

Everything that happened since that long-ago night of proud self-pity in my kitchen, had been directed by my loving Father. He knew it was necessary for me to learn some things before I could grow any farther with Him.

One lesson was very clear to me now: Commitment to any calling means you lose something—the freedom of unlimited choices. But commitment also means you gain a deep sense of purpose and belonging that can't be had without boundaries.

"Excuse me sir, but that happens to be my wife you're cuddling. I must ask you to remove yourself at once, or I shall be forced to take action!"

I ventured to raise one lazy lid to look sideways at my husband. He'd stood up behind me, and reaching over, took Ted by one fuzzy ear. He tugged Kit's big bear out of my embrace.

"You know I can't go home without Ted in my arms," I protested.

Joe deposited Ted at the end of the little bench, and swung his long legs over to sit beside me.

"Or you in mine," he smiled, and made good on his promise.

THE END

# GLOSSARY OF FOREIGN TERMS

| | |
|---|---|
| **Abd-el-** | servant of |
| **Aid el Kebir** | Spring rite commemorating Abraham's willingness to sacrifice Isaac |
| **Aït** | children of (a tribe) |
| **Ackbar** | elder |
| **Alems** | plural of Ulama |
| **Atai benaana** | mint tea |
| **Bab** | monumental gate |
| **Babouche** | pointed slippers worn inside a Moroccan home |
| **Balek** | "Attention" or "Look Out" |
| **Bali** | ancient |
| **Bidonville** | shantytown |
| **Bilad al siba** | "Land of Insolence" or "Land of Dissidence" |
| **Bstila** | stuffed pancake |
| **Buaû** | a witch with goat's feet |
| **Caravanserai** | an inn for caravans |
| **Chergui** | strong, dry, dusty wind |
| **Choukhara** | Moroccan leather holdall, worn over the shoulder |
| **Couscous** | boiled grain |
| **Dar** | castle |
| **Doaur** | farming hamlet |
| **Dirhams** | Moroccan currency |
| **Djebel** | mountain |
| **Djellaba** | garment, shapeless, with sleeves and hood; often home-spun and striped |
| **Djenina** | courtyard garden |
| **El Jamaâ** | Friday, the regular Muslim holy day of Assembly |

| | |
|---|---|
| **El Maghreb el Aksa** | The Land of Setting Sun or the Land Farthest West |
| **Fantasias** | horse racing |
| **Fatiha** | First surah of the Koran |
| **Fez-el-Bali** | Old Fez |
| **Fez-Jedid** | New Fez |
| **Fqihs** | Muslim schoolteachers |
| **Gallasha** | woman who prepares new bride before and after wedding |
| **Guedra** | wild, erotic dance of Blue Men |
| **Had** | one or Sunday |
| **Hadith** | saying |
| **Hadj** | trip to Mecca or name given to one who has accomplished it |
| **Haik** | tent-like white garment worn by Muslim women |
| **Hammada** | stony desert |
| **Harira** | thick vegetable soup |
| **Hezzabs** | endlessly recite Koran |
| **Horm** | place of asylum, "Haven" |
| **Imam** | prayer or religious leader |
| **Inch'Allah** | if God wills |
| **Jinn** | invisible, evil genies residing in earth, trees or animals (plural Jinnis) |
| **Kab el ghzal** | croissant stuffed with crushed almonds and rolled in powdered sugar |
| **Kanun** | 3-legged charcoal burner |
| **Kasbah** | citadel or fortified house |
| **Kesrah** | Moroccan bread |
| **Khatib** | preachers (Friday sermon) or prayer leader |
| **Kif** | marijuana or hashish |

| | |
|---|---|
| **Koubba** | small, white, domed tomb of a saintly man |
| **Ksour** | fortified Saharan village |
| **Lalla** | title of a woman of noble birth |
| **Maghreb** | where the sun sets, i.e. Northwest Africa (used to denote Tunisia, Algeria & Morocco) |
| **Marabouts** | village holy men |
| **Maroc** | resident of Morocco |
| **Masihi** | Christians |
| **Medina** | medieval part of the city |
| **Medrassa** | Muslim law and theological college |
| **Minaret** | tower on a mosque from which faithful are called to prayer |
| **Misbahas** | prayer beads or "worry beads" |
| **Mosque** | Islamic place of worship |
| **Moukkala** | heavily-encrusted Moroccan rifle |
| **Moussems** | annual pilgrimage, accompanied by festivities |
| **Muezzin** | those that call the faithful to prayer |
| **Nafaqua** | Islamic law requiring husband to provide for wife or wives |
| **Oued** | river |
| **Pasha** | title of person of high rank |
| **Piste** | country road |
| **Polisarios** | shortened title, in French, for Sharawi Popular Liberation Army |
| **R'Guibats** | nomadic herders |
| **Ras el Am** | New Year's day |
| **Razzia** | raid or siege |

| | |
|---|---|
| Rue | Street |
| Salaam | "Peace," used as greeting, also the bow of greeting |
| Salah | worship |
| Scirrocos | see Chergui |
| Sebt | Saturday or 7 |
| Serwhals | pants worn by the mountain villagers |
| Sharawi | traditional inhabitants of Western Sahara |
| Shari 'a | traditional codes of Islamic law |
| Shiek | chieftan |
| Shoukran | "Thank you" |
| Souk | market |
| Souk-el-Sebt | Saturday market |
| sultana | sultan's or chieftain's wife |
| Sûreté | police/intelligence agency |
| Tajin | meat dish cooked slowly in sauce |
| Tarboosh | red fez |
| Tía | aunt |
| Tizi | high mountain pass |
| Tleta | three or Tuesday |
| Touareg | desert nomads of Berber origin (the Blue People) |
| ulama | teacher of Muslim law |
| Ville Nouvelle | Newest city |
| Yallah | "Let's go" |
| yashmak | double full-face veil worn by married women |
| Zankat | street |
| Zellig | Moorish decorative tile |